Haydn Richards

Junior Englisn 2

New Edition

Ginn is an imprint of Pearson Education Limited, a company incorporated in England and Wales, having its registered office at Edinburgh Gate, Harlow, Essex, CM20 2JE. Registered company number: 872828

www.pearsonglobalschools.com

Text © Haydn Richards, 1965

Revised edition 1997
This edition 2008

20 19 18 17 16 15
IMP: 20 19 18 17 16

British Library Cataloguing in Publication Data is available from the British Library on request.

ISBN 978 0 435996 83 3

Typeset and illustrated by Planman Technologies India Pvt. Ltd.
Original illustrations © Pearson Education Ltd, 2008
Cover design by Tony Richardson
Cover illustration © Pearson Education Ltd, 2008
Printed by Multivista Global Ltd

Acknowledgements
Every effort has been made to contact copyright holders of material reproduced in this book. Any omissions will be rectified in subsequent printings if notice is given to the publishers.

page 12 **Raman meets the rocking-horse**
The Rocking-Horse by Rosemary Manning.
By kind permission of Hamish Hamilton Ltd.

page 18 **Some useful finds**
The Bicycle Wheel by Ruth Ainsworth.
By kind permission of Hamish Hamilton Ltd.

page 24 **Magic balloons**
My First Science Book by Angela Wilkes, published by Dorling Kindersley.
By kind permission of Dorling Kindersley Holdings plc.

page 30 **Lone Dog**
"Lone Dog" by Irene Rutherford McLeod, from *Songs to Save a Soul* by Irene Rutherford McLeod, published by Chatto and Windus.
By kind permission of the Estate of Irene Rutherford McLeod.

page 78 **Feeding the Cats**
"Feeding the Cats" © Fleur Adcock.
By kind permission of Fleur Adcock.

page 84 **A bear cub's adventure**
Baby Mishook by Leon Golschmann.
By kind permission of Bodley Head.

PREFACE

This new edition of Haydn Richards' popular series is for pupils studying in primary schools. Based on the revised 1997 edition, this new edition retains the excellent coverage of spelling, punctuation and grammar topics in each of the four books, as well as the wide range and varying complexity of the reading comprehension and vocabulary exercises.

In this new edition, key spelling, punctuation and grammar points (and examples of these) are always highlighted in boxes on the page for quick and easy reference.

The Publisher

CONTENTS

NOUNS: NAMING WORDS

The dog followed the boy.

Dog is the **name** of an animal. **Boy** is the **name** of a person.

A **noun** is the name of a **person** or thing.

Ⓐ Find the nouns in these sentences. Write them in your book.

1 The window was broken.		**6** The sea beat against the rocks.	
2 I lost my knife.		**7** The dog barked at the postman.	
3 This pencil is too short.		**8** Summer is the warmest season.	
4 The cake was stale.		**9** The plane landed safely.	
5 The bird flew away.		**10** Only one apple was left in the dish.	

Ⓑ Name three things you might find in these places. Use your dictionary.

1 a toy shop	**3** a kitchen	**5** a car	**7** a cinema
2 a farmyard	**4** a railway station	**6** a hospital	**8** a church

VERBS: DOING WORDS

> *The butcher cut the meat and weighed it.*
>
> The words **cut** and **weighed** tell us what the butcher **did** to the meat.
>
> These are **doing** words, or **action** words.
>
> A **verb** is a word that shows **action**.

A Find the verbs in these sentences. Write them in your book.

1 The little girl cried.
2 We cut a lot of wood for the fire.
3 Please pass me the jam.
4 Roy knocked at the door of the office.
5 Two robins hopped on to the window-ledge.
6 Preshani put her toys away and went to bed.
7 After school John cycles to the park and plays cricket.
8 The clown smiled when we waved to him.
9 Harry broke his arm when he fell off his bicycle.
10 Kirsty ate four sweets and gave the rest away.

B Name three actions which might be done by each of these people.

Example   a baby   cry, play, suck

1 a doctor
2 a footballer
3 your teacher
4 a gardener
5 a cricketer
6 a policeman
7 a pupil in your class
8 a farmer

VOWELS

Instead of **a** always write **an** before words beginning with

a   **e**   **i**   **o**   **u**.

These letters are called **vowels**.

acorn	apron	arrow	eel	eye	orange
anchor	arch	axe	egg	island	orchard
apple	arm	easel	envelope	oar	

(A) Write the names of these things, putting **an** before each.
You will find them in the list above.

(B) Write **a** or **an** before each of these words.

1 _____ book   9 _____ chair
2 _____ ant   10 _____ organ
3 _____ apple   11 _____ ox
4 _____ rock   12 _____ elf
5 _____ oval   13 _____ sweet
6 _____ egg   14 _____ hat
7 _____ flag   15 _____ imp
8 _____ inn   16 _____ shoe

(C) Write **a** or **an** to finish the sentences.

1 Pauline ate _____ apple and _____ banana.
2 I will give you _____ invitation tomorrow.
3 We came to _____ lake with _____ island in the middle.
4 Lucy is spending _____ holiday with _____ aunt in London.
5 _____ east wind is colder than _____ west wind.

VERBS: ADDING -ed AND -ing

(A) Write **-ing** after each word.

1 look	**4** teach	**7** read
2 walk	**5** pay	**8** camp
3 push	**6** go	**9** wear

(B) Write **-ed** after each word.

1 stay	**4** rush	**7** fill
2 post	**5** touch	**8** end
3 work	**6** help	**9** turn

(C) Write **-ing** after each word.
Drop the **e** at the end.

Example   serve   serving

1 blaze	**4** love	**7** raise
2 dance	**5** share	**8** hope
3 dare	**6** waste	

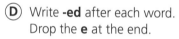

(D) Write **-ed** after each word.
Drop the **e** at the end.

Example   place   placed

1 taste	**4** hate	**7** snore
2 live	**5** chase	**8** close
3 rattle	**6** blame	

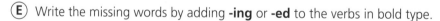

(E) Write the missing words by adding **-ing** or **-ed** to the verbs in bold type.

1 We saw a small dog _____ a cat.   **chase**
2 The fire _____ when a log was put on it.   **blaze**
3 The old man was _____ most of the night.   **snore**
4 Nobody _____ to answer the door.   **dare**
5 Paul sat on the rug _____ the cat.   **stroke**
6 We got there just as the shop was _____.   **close**

ADJECTIVES: DESCRIBING WORDS

The team wore red shirts.

The word **red** tells us **what kind** of **shirts** the team wore.

Because it describes the noun **shirts**, we call it an **adjective**.

An **adjective** is a word that describes a **noun**.

Examples

loud	*sharp*	*tidy*	*white*	*heavy*
savage	*juicy*	*leather*	*deep*	*beautiful*

(A) Pick out and write the adjectives in these sentences.

1 A big lorry was parked outside the school.
2 The sky became very dark before the storm broke.
3 Claire wore a new dress at the party.
4 The baby was playing with a huge teddy bear.
5 The torch gave a brilliant light.
6 The captain of the ship had a wooden leg.
7 They made an easy crossing of the shallow river.
8 We helped the blind man across the road.
9 It was such a busy street.
10 You always think you're so clever.

(B) Choose an adjective from the list above to fill each of the spaces below.

1 a _____ doll	5 a _____ load	9 a _____ sheet
2 a _____ knife	6 a _____ pear	10 a _____ cut
3 a _____ noise	7 a _____ belt	
4 a _____ dog	8 a _____ room	

CINDERELLA

Cinderella ran to the garden and brought her godmother the finest pumpkin she could find, wondering how this would help her to go to the ball.

The godmother scooped out the inside of the pumpkin, leaving nothing but the rind. Then she touched it with her magic wand, and the pumpkin was changed in a moment into a fine coach, all shining with gold.

After that she went to look into the mouse-trap, where she found six mice, all alive. She told Cinderella to lift the trap-door up a little, and as each mouse came out she gave it a tap with her wand. At once it was changed into a beautiful horse. This made a very fine team of six horses, all dappled grey in colour.

Tales from Perrault

1 Where did Cinderella find the pumpkin?
2 What happened when her godmother touched the pumpkin with her wand?
3 What happened to the mice when she tapped them with the wand?
4 What is another word for **rind**?
5 Does **dappled** mean
  a smooth and silky?
  b having spots and patches of a different colour?
  c striped like a tabby cat?

QUESTIONS

Every question must have a **question mark (?)** at the end.
Why were you so late?
Where have you been?

why	who	how	what	whose
have	when	did	which	where

(A) Use the words in the list above to fill the spaces in the questions below. Remember to put a question mark (?) at the end of each question.

1 _____ you enjoy the tea
2 _____ are you today
3 _____ told you about the party
4 _____ were you absent yesterday
5 _____ did you have for dinner
6 _____ are you coming to see me
7 _____ of these books do you like best
8 _____ has Mum put the sweets
9 _____ cap is this
10 _____ you been to London

(B) Write five sentences of your own, each beginning with one of the words from the list above.

(C) Copy these sentences. Put a full stop at the end of each statement and a question mark at the end of each question.

1 I have lost my anorak
2 Did you find your cat
3 Are you feeling all right
4 Ling is a vegetarian
5 Does anyone know today's date
6 Can you help me
7 Donna collects matchboxes

THE WEATHER

breezy	*icy*
windy	*sunny*
stormy	*showery*
misty	*rainy*
foggy	*thundery*

When the weather is wet,
We must not fret.
When the weather is cold,
We must not scold.
When the weather is warm
We must not storm,
But be thankful together
Whatever the weather.

(A) The words in the box above are used to describe weather. Write these sentences in your book, filling each space with a word from the box.

    1 When the wind is blowing hard it is _____.
    2 When the sun is shining it is _____.
    3 When there is a fog it is _____.
    4 When there is a mist it is _____.
    5 When the rain pours it is a _____ day.
    6 When there is a storm it is _____.
    7 When there is a breeze it is _____.
    8 When there is thunder it is _____.
    9 When there are showers the weather is _____.
  10 When the wind is as cold as ice it is _____.

(B) Write two or three sentences about any two of these.

    1 a sunny morning   **4** a windy day
    2 a cold afternoon   **5** a stormy sea
    3 a wet afternoon   **6** a foggy night

showeryfoggyicysunnywindy

USING THE RIGHT WORD

has	have
James **has** two pet rats.	Cats **have** whiskers.
one	more than one
did	**done**
He **did** his work well.	He **has done** his work well.
	helping word: **has**
is	**are**
This apple **is** sour.	These apples **are** sour.
one	more than one
was	**were**
The boy **was** happy.	The boys **were** happy.
one	more than one
saw	**seen**
We **saw** the Tower of London.	We **have seen** the Tower of London.
	helping word: **have**

(A) Choose the right word from the pair above to fill each space.

1	has	have	He can't run because he _____ a bad leg.
2	was	were	The boy _____ afraid of the bull.
3	was	were	Several cows _____ grazing in the field.
4	did	done	They have _____ everything I asked them to do.
5	is	are	Chung _____ a very kind boy.
6	saw	seen	I have never _____ an eclipse of the sun.

(B) Write the word that will fill each gap.

1	saw	seen	Three people _____ the accident.
2	did	done	Rania _____ her best to tidy the garage.
3	is	are	The book _____ kept on the shelf.
4	did	done	Philip rested when he had _____ his work.
5	saw	seen	It is the biggest trout I have _____.
6	is	are	The books _____ kept on the shelf.

HOMONYMS: WORDS WITH MORE THAN ONE MEANING

Some words have more than one meaning. They are called **homonyms**.

*The brown **bear** climbed the tree.*
*Sandra could hardly **bear** the pain.*

bark	chest	kind	match	shed
blow	fair	light	ring	watch

Use the words in the list above to fill the spaces in the sentences. The same word must be used for each pair of sentences.

1 The lawn mower is kept in the garden _____.
 Many trees _____ their leaves in the autumn.
2 The _____ woman put £1 in the collecting box.
 This is a different _____ of toffee.
3 It is time to _____ the school bell.
 The wedding _____ was made of solid gold.
4 The oak tree has a rough _____ .
 The dog began to _____ when the children teased him.
5 Much damage is done when high winds _____.
 A _____ on the head knocked the boxer out.
6 Sara has very _____ hair.
 There were many amusements at the _____.
7 My new _____ keeps very good time.
 We did not _____ television last night.
8 The parcel was as _____ as a feather.
 The bedside lamp gave out lots of _____.
9 There was a big crowd at the football _____.
 Grandad struck a _____ and lit his pipe.
10 James has a cold on his _____.
 The tools are kept in a big wooden _____.

USING CAPITAL LETTERS

Capital letters are used:

to begin a sentence	***A**lways start a sentence with a capital letter.*
for the names of people and pets	***G**eorge, **J**ennifer, **F**luffy, **P**ongo* *Also for **M**r, **M**rs, **D**r*
for the names of places, rivers,	***B**ristol, **T**hames, **S**nowdon, **A**tlantic*
mountains, and so on for addresses	*29 **S**outh **R**oad, Barnsdale, **BA**12 3**QT***
for the names of the days of the week	***M**onday, **W**ednesday, **S**aturday*
for the word 'I'	***I** did my best but **I** failed.*

Copy these sentences, using capital letters where they are needed.

1 henry chaplin lives in hastings.
2 the national gallery has some beautiful paintings.
3 david and i are going to london for a day.
4 we hope to go next friday.
5 the highest mountain in wales is snowdon.
6 canterbury is in kent.
7 a new shop has opened in bond street.
8 my mother and i are going to australia in july.
9 colin has a pet dog named pepper.
10 we paid a visit to mr and mrs sandhu.

RAMAN MEETS THE ROCKING-HORSE

Raman asked his mother after school if he could go home and play with Jock. She said, "Yes," and she would come and fetch him at half-past five. She wore a long, flowing sari, and Jock thought she was very beautiful.

"She's an Indian princess," he thought. "I'll ride to her rescue if she's in danger."

When they reached Jock's house, Jock took Raman into the basement room, and went up to the horse and patted his neck.

"What's he called?" asked Raman, gazing at the horse with admiration.

"I don't know yet," answered Jock and added quickly: "At least I do, but his name's a secret. He only allows *me* to call him by it."

This was not quite true, as Jock hadn't yet invented a name for him, but he knew that he would sometime.

"He's wonderful," breathed Raman. "Can I have a ride?"

"Well, he doesn't like strangers much," answered Jock. "I'll ride him first so that he can look at you and get used to you."

The Rocking-Horse by Rosemary Manning

1 At what time of day did Raman go to play with Jock?
2 What is a **sari**?
3 What is the difference between **gazing** and **looking**?
4 Why did Jock think of Raman's mother as a princess?
5 In what part of the house was the rocking-horse kept?
6 What reason did Jock give Raman for not telling him the horse's name?
7 What was Jock's real reason for not telling him?
8 What reason did Jock give Raman for having the first ride himself?

HERE AND HEAR; THERE AND THEIR

Here means **in this place.**
*I left the bag **here** five minutes ago.*

Hear is what you do with your ears.
*We could **hear** the thrushes singing.*

There means **in that place.**
*He lives over **there**.*

Their means **belonging to them.**
*The boys played with **their** football.*

(A) Write **here** or **hear** in each space.

1 Will you stay _____ till I come back?
2 Ann did not _____ her mother calling her.
3 We could _____ someone snoring in the next room.
4 _____ is the ball you were looking for.
5 Would you like to live _____?
6 Deaf people cannot _____.

(B) Write **there** or **their** in each space.

1 The children gave _____ dog a bath.
2 I waited _____ for nearly an hour.
3 _____ are a hundred pence in a pound.
4 Is _____ room for me to sit down?
5 The two boys went to the show with _____ cousin.
6 I saw patches of clover here and _____ on the lawn.
7 He said he left the parcel _____ and now it's gone.
8 We looked here, _____ , and everywhere.
9 _____ excuse for being late was ridiculous.

PLURALS

Singular means **one**.
Plural means **more than one**.

Examples

Singular	*boy*	*glass*	*daisy*	*leaf*
Plural	*boys*	*glasses*	*daisies*	*leaves*

leaf

(A) Add **-s** to each word to form the plural.

1 bird   **4** farmer   **7** river
2 cook   **5** tree   **8** coat
3 head   **6** chair

(B) Add **-es** to each word to form the plural.

1 bush   **4** brush   **7** church
2 bunch   **5** box   **8** match
3 coach   **6** dish

(C) Change **y** to i and add **-es**.

1 fly   **4** berry   **7** city
2 pony   **5** story   **8** penny
3 coach   **6** lady

(D) Change **f** to **v** and add **-es**.

1 elf   **4** half   **7** wolf
2 shelf   **5** calf   **8** sheaf
3 loaf   **6** leaf

(E) Copy these sentences, making each noun in bold type plural.

Example **1** *They fed the **calves** on milk.*

1 They fed the **calf** on milk.
2 The **butcher** sharpened the **knife**.
3 The **baker** put the burnt **loaf** on the **shelf**.
4 The **gardener** trimmed the **bush**.
5 The **elf** stitched the **shoe**.
6 The **leaf** fell from the **tree**.
7 The **fly** buzzed round the **baby**.
8 The **girl** put the **penny** in the **box**.

leaves

VERBS: ADDING -ed AND -ing

> When we add **-ed** or **-ing** to each of the words in this list we double the last letter.
>
> *Examples*
>
> | nod | hum | drop | grin |
> |---|---|---|---|
> | nod**ded** | hum**med** | drop**ped** | grin**ned** |
> | nod**ding** | hum**ming** | drop**ping** | grin**ning** |

(A) Add **-ing** to each word, first doubling the last letter.

1 peg	**6** skim
2 chat	**7** drop
3 rob	**8** skid
4 stab	**9** drag
5 hum	**10** slip

(B) Add **-ed** to each word, first doubling the last letter.

1 snap	**6** dip
2 grin	**7** trim
3 lap	**8** grab
4 rub	**9** slam
5 nod	**10** drip

(C) Fill each space with the right verb.

1 Water was _____ from a hole in the can.

2 The car _____ on the wet road and crashed.

3 Joy _____ a merry tune as she went along.

4 Mum _____ the wet clothes on the line.

5 The rude boy _____ the door as he went out.

6 Jean-Paul _____ on a banana skin and hurt his leg.

7 The gardener was busy _____ the hedge.

8 A lovely white kitten was _____ a saucer of milk.

THE END STOPS

A **full stop** is put at the end of every statement.

I hung my coat on the coat-hanger.

A **question mark** is put at the end of every question.

Did you hang your coat on the coat-hanger?

An **exclamation mark** is put at the end of every shouted command.

Put that down at once!

Full stops, question marks and exclamation marks are all **end stops**.

(A) Copy each sentence. Put a full stop, a question mark or an exclamation mark at the end of each.

   1 The bushy tail of a fox is called a brush
   2 A camel can go for days without water
   3 Have you visited the Tower of London
   4 The Nile is a long river in Africa
   5 Don't you dare do that
   6 Will you call for me in the morning
   7 Our school starts at nine o'clock
   8 Did you post the letter I gave you
   9 Beavers can gnaw through big trees
10 Put that down immediately
11 Are you sorry you are leaving Liverpool
12 Just go away

(B) Write two statements, two questions and two commands. Remember to use the correct end stop.

FORMING NOUNS

Some nouns are formed by adding **-ness** to words.

sad	*slow*	*deaf*	*stout*
sad**ness**	slow**ness**	deaf**ness**	stout**ness**

When **-ness** is added to words ending with **y**, the **y** is changed to **i**.

steady	*shabby*	*sleepy*
stead**iness**	shabb**iness**	sleep**iness**

Ⓐ Add **-ness** to these words.

1 glad	**4** tired	**7** lame	**10** fresh	**13** giddy
2 stale	**5** loud	**8** blind	**11** sore	**14** wicked
3 happy	**6** greedy	**9** rough	**12** sad	**15** good

Ⓑ Fill each space with the noun formed from the word in bold type.

1 Jennie thanked her teacher for her _____. **kind**
2 The wolves started to howl as _____ fell. **dark**
3 Winter often brings much _____. **ill**
4 It is _____ to speed on busy roads. **mad**
5 The wood was two centimetres in _____. **thick**
6 The old man was suffering from _____. **giddy**
7 We were surprised at the _____ of the squirrels. **tame**
8 The man's _____ was caused by an explosion. **deaf**
9 Mrs Platt scolded Ben for his _____. **lazy**
10 Chandra was dazzled by the _____ of the sun. **bright**

SOME USEFUL FINDS

Just then the rubbish dump came into sight, and they started to run towards it. It was a flattish hill of ashes and cinders, mixed with old tyres and broken furniture.

James and Jenny began to climb over this hill of rubbish, exclaiming every time they found a treasure. Penny followed, not liking the dust that rose under her feet, and the crunch of the cinders, but was as pleased as the others when she found a big bundle of paper with one side plain.

"Drawing paper!" she called out. "Scribbling paper! Sheets and sheets and sheets. We can make it pretty, and paper the whole of the dolls' house. We can play schools, too."

"A chain," said James, clanking it joyfully. "A strong, useful chain. We can play at prisons and I'll chain you up."

The Bicycle Wheel by Ruth Ainsworth

1 What four things did the rubbish dump consist of?
2 Explain what is meant by the word **treasure** in this passage.
3 What did James and Jenny do every time they found a treasure?
4 What two things did Penny not like about the dump?
5 What made Penny pleased when she looked through the dump?
6 What three things did Penny want to do with the paper?
7 What is the difference between **shaking** a chain and **clanking** it?
8 James used two adjectives to describe the chain. What are they?
9 What did he suggest they did with it?
10 How do you think the children felt as they climbed over the dump?

ADJECTIVES: DESCRIBING WORDS

Adjectives can be formed by adding **-y** to some words.

Examples   *rust*   *wealth*   *greed*   *storm*
                 *rust**y***   *wealth**y***   *greed**y***   *storm**y***

When **-y** is added to some words the last letter of the word is doubled.

Examples   *sun*   *fur*   *mud*   *fog*   *sand*
                 *sun**ny***   *fur**ry***   *mud**dy***   *fog**gy***   *san**dy***

When **-y** is added to a word ending with **e** this letter is dropped.

Examples   *nois**e***   *shad**e***   *eas**e***   *smok**e***   *ston**e***
                 *nois**y***   *shad**y***   *eas**y***   *smok**y***   *ston**y***

(A) What are the missing words?

1 Hands covered with dirt   _____ hands
2 A day of strong winds   a _____ day
3 A mountain with many rocks   a _____ mountain
4 A beach covered with sand   a _____ beach
5 A table covered with dust   a _____ table
6 A chest covered with hair   a _____ chest
7 Hair that has curls   _____ hair
8 Food that has a lot of salt   _____ food
9 A sky with many clouds   a _____ sky
10 A girl who has lots of luck   a _____ girl

(B) What are the missing adjectives?

1 a _____ day   **sun**
2 an _____ exercise   **ease**
3 a _____ morning   **mist**
4 a _____ animal   **fur**
5 a _____ chimney   **smoke**
6 a _____ class   **noise**
7 a _____ drink   **fizz**
8 a _____ tree   **shade**
9 a _____ path   **stone**
10 a _____ night   **fog**
11 a _____ line   **wave**
12 a _____ joke   **fun**
13 a _____ face   **spot**
14 a _____ pupil   **laze**
15 a _____ lane   **mud**

VERBS: ADDING -es AND -ed

When **-es** or **-ed** is added to a verb ending with **y**, this letter is first changed to **i**.

*I **try** hard.*

*He **tries** hard.*

*She **tried** hard.*

(A) Copy and fill in the missing letters.

1 try	_ _ _ es	**6** dirty	_ _ _ _ _ es
2 cry	_ _ _ ed	**7** copy	_ _ _ _ _ ed
3 dry	_ _ _ ed	**8** empty	_ _ _ _ _ es
4 fry	_ _ _ es	**9** hurry	_ _ _ _ _ ed
5 spy	_ _ _ ed	**10** carry	_ _ _ _ _ es

(B) Finish each sentence by using the right form of the verb in bold type, adding **-es** or **-ed** as needed.

1 Rushkana is ____ every morning that she will miss the bus. **worry**

2 Every day Ann ____ sums from Soraya. **copy**

3 She ____ because she had cut her knee. **cry**

4 Although we ____ to the station we missed the train. **hurry**

5 Again and again the little spider ____ to climb up the thread. **try**

6 David ____ his books to school in a satchel. **carry**

7 Every time she washes her hands she ____ them well. **dry**

8 Yesterday the dustmen ____ all the bins in our street. **empty**

9 I ____ an owl up the church tower. **spy**

10 My mother says that she ____ people with curly hair. **envy**

HOMOPHONES: SAME SOUND, DIFFERENT MEANING

Some words have the same sound as other words, but they are different in spelling and meaning. They are called **homophones**.

bare   A **bare** tree has no leaves.
bear   The polar **bear** is a very big animal.

dear   The dress was too **dear** so she did not buy it.
          Jane is a very **dear** friend of mine.
deer   A **deer** is a graceful animal.

fair   **fair** hair is light in colour.
          We had fun at the **fair**.
fare   The bus conductor asked me for my **fare**.

heel   The back part of your foot is called the **heal**.
heal   To **heal** people means to make them well.

dear
dear
de—r
deer
deer

Choose the correct word from the pairs in the box to complete each sentence.

1 fair   fare
The bus _____ to school is fifty pence.

2 heel   heal
The cut on your finger will soon _____.

3 bear   bare
The big brown _____ sat up and begged.

4 heel   heal
The _____ of the woman's shoe came right off.

5 fair   fare
Peter won a coconut at the _____.

6 bear   bare
Many trees are _____ in winter.

7 dear   deer
We saw ten _____ in the park.

PUNCTUATION

Putting full stops, commas, question marks, etc., in sentences is called **punctuation**.

1 A full stop is used to end a sentence that makes a statement.
Gold is mined in South Africa.

2 A question mark is used to end a sentence that asks a question.
How many days are there in a week?

3 An exclamation mark is used after a word or a sentence that is spoken excitedly, and after shouted commands.
Run! The tide's coming in fast!

4 Commas are used:
a to separate the name of a person directly spoken to from the rest of the sentence.
Richard, have you locked the door?
Have you locked the door, Richard?
b to separate words in a list when **and** or **or** is used to separate the last two words only.
Gold, iron, silver and lead are all metals.
c after words like **well**, **oh**, **yes**, **no** and **now** when they begin a sentence.
Well, I warned you not to do it.
d to set off the word **please** at the end of a sentence.
Have you the right time, please?

Insert punctuation marks where necessary in these sentences.

1 Have you ever spent a holiday abroad
2 Yes I went to Spain last summer
3 Please lock up before you go Philip
4 Jennifer have you finished your homework
5 Cyprus Corsica Malta Elba and Sicily are all islands

SYNONYMS

a **wealthy** man

a **rich** man

The words **wealthy** and **rich** have much the same meaning.

Learn the list of synonyms before answering the questions.

collect	gather
difficult	hard
pile	heap
commence	begin
hasten	hurry
peril	danger
weeping	crying
drowsy	sleepy
naked	bare
plucky	brave

(A) Write a simpler word in place of each word in bold type.

1 The concert will **commence** at 7 o'clock.
2 Janine found the sum very **difficult**.
3 The ship was in great **peril**.
4 A **pile** of stones lay outside the school.
5 The **plucky** sailor saved the boy's life.
6 At the funeral several people were **weeping**.
7 Sitting near a big fire makes one **drowsy**.
8 The sun shone on the swimmer's **naked** back.

(B) In each group below select the word that is similar in meaning to the word in bold type.

1 **drowsy**	2 **hasten**	3 **collect**
lively	fix	give
quick	hurry	spend
active	work	gather
sleepy	play	climb

4 **difficult**	5 **peril**	6 **plucky**
clever	danger	silly
easy	length	brave
hard	safety	short
simple	depth	noisy

7 **assist**	8 **halt**	9 **feeble**
help	hurry	loving
coax	linger	weak
hinder	run	silly
wait	stop	famous

MAGIC BALLOONS

You will need two balloons, a little sugar and a sheet of paper torn into small pieces.

1 Blow up the balloons. You may need an adult to help you do this. Tie the end of each balloon into a firm knot.
2 Now rub each balloon hard against your sweater. The trick works best if the sweater you are wearing is made of wool.
3 Hold one balloon just above the torn pieces of paper. What happens? Then try holding a balloon just above some sugar.

The balloons pick up the torn up paper and sugar, as if by magic.

Rubbing a balloon against wool charges it with static electricity. This gives the balloon enough magnetic power to pick up very light things, like the paper and sugar. It also makes the paper and sugar stick to the balloon.

Most things contain static electricity. You cannot see it, but you can rub it off one thing and on to another, making it static.

From *My First Science Book* by Angela Wilkes

1 What can you make the balloons do after you have rubbed them against a woollen sweater?
2 What is making the balloons pick up the paper and sugar?
3 Why are paper and sugar good things to use in the experiment?
4 We are seeing an **invisible** force at work in this experiment.
   What does **invisible** mean?
5 **Magic** balloons? True or false? Explain.
6 Find a word in the passage that begins with a silent letter.
7 Find a word in the passage that rhymes with **try**.
8 Find three words in the passage that end with **-ic**.

FUN WITH WORDS

In each column in Exercise A below there are two pairs of words and one odd word.

You have to find the word that will make up the third pair.

Look at the first pair of words: *ear   hear*

The second word is made by adding the letter **h** to the beginning of the first word.

Look at the second pair: *at   hat*

The second word is again formed by writing **h** before the first word.

To find the missing word write **h** before the odd word.

Example arm   harm

(A) Now find the other missing words. In every column a different letter must be added.

1 ear	hear	**3** all	ball	**5** ark	park
at	hat	eat	beat	ink	pink
arm	_____	oil	_____	lay	_____

2 ill	mill	**4** old	gold
ask	mask	lad	glad
other	_____	race	_____

(B) In each line below the same letter ends the first word and begins the second. Write the ten pairs of words.

Example   **1**   *sat   tea*

1 sa _	_ ea	**6** pos _	_ rap
2 be _	_ og	**7** fil _	_ ift
3 sh _	_ gg	**8** goo _	_ oor
4 bi _	_ un	**9** hea _	_ ich
5 wa _	_ ly	**10** hel _	_ lay

(C) Test your word power. Can you supply the missing letters? All the words end in **-ic**.

1 When the chain was shaken, it made a me _ _ _ _ ic noise.
2 My parents were fr _ _ _ ic with worry when I came home late.
3 Keep calm and don't pa _ ic.
4 How can you charge a balloon with st _ _ ic electricity?
5 Wash that cut carefully or it will turn se _ _ ic.

SHOWING OWNERSHIP

I like Simon's new puppy. The **'s** in Simon's shows that the puppy **belongs** to Simon. It is **his**. He **owns** it	*the kite that belongs to Paul (long way)* *Paul's kite (short way)* *the wool of the sheep (long way)* *the sheep's wool (short way)*

(A) Copy these into your book, putting in the ' before the **s**.

1 the robin s breast
2 the sailor s cap
3 the horse s mane
4 the rabbit s tail
5 the old man s beard

6 the cashier s till
7 the lady s handbag
8 the sheep s wool
9 the Queen s crown
10 the dog s collar

(B) Write these the short way.

1 the book belonging to Mary

2 the bat that belongs to Peter

3 the ribbon belonging to Ann

4 the watch that belongs to Dad

5 the ring that belongs to Mum

(C) Write these the short way.

1 the fur of the cat

2 the den of the lion

3 the beak of the blackbird

4 the ears of the donkey

5 the horns of the cow

OPPOSITES USING *un-*

Safe   Unsafe

Some words are given an opposite meaning by writing **un-** before them.

Look at the words above the pictures.

(A) Form the opposites of these words by using **un-**.

1 happy	**5** do	**9** roll
2 willing	**6** screw	**10** real
3 paid	**7** tie	**11** safe
4 seen	**8** wise	**12** steady

(B) Choose any six of the words you have made and use them in sentences of your own.

(C) Copy these sentences, adding **un-** to the words in bold type to give them an opposite meaning.

1 The new road is **finished**.
2 The doctor said that Martin was very **healthy**.
3 The pears were **ripe**.
4 The referee was **fair** in what he said.
5 Janine was **kind** to animals.
6 Dad could not **lock** the car.
7 The gym had an **even** floor.
8 The man was **known** to the police.

ALPHABETICAL ORDER

**abcd
efgh
ijklm
nopq
rstuv
wxyz**

(A) Look at the alphabet.

1 Write the third letter of the alphabet.
2 Which letter is last but one?
3 Which letter comes between **j** and **l**?
4 What are the missing letters?

g   h   _   j   k   _   m   n   o   _   q

(B) Write each group of words in **abc** or alphabetical order. Look at the first letter of each word.

1 head	2 look	3 green
train	ready	water
before	winter	cross
food	another	idea
also	small	pull

4 paint	5 please
teach	answer
little	mountain
heart	young
alone	under

(C) In each group below all the words are in alphabetical order except one. Write the odd word in each group.

Example **1** *bicycle*

1 night	2 army	3 early
orange	bread	dress
pretty	colour	figure
queen	letter	garden
bicycle	doctor	house

4 kitchen	5 beauty
length	ground
window	middle
mouse	season
north	heavy

SHORT FORMS

You have learnt how to join two words, one of which is **not**.

is not	*isn't*	*does not*	*doesn't*
was not	*wasn't*	*has not*	*hasn't*

Notice that the ' stands for the **o** that is left out.

We can also join **is** to another word in this way.

he is	*he's*	*that is*	*that's*
she is	*she's*	*what is*	*what's*
it is	*it's*	*where is*	*where's*
who is	*who's*	*there is*	*there's*

Remember that the **'** stands for the **i** that is left out.

Write these sentences, joining the two words in bold type in each.

 1 Brian says **he is** too busy to play.
 2 I think **that is** a lovely dress.
 3 Clare is tall, and **she is** pretty, too.
 4 Thank goodness **it is** a fine day.
 5 We can't work when **there is** a noise in the room.
 6 I can guess **what is** in the box.
 7 I wonder **who is** going to the party tonight.
 8 **It is** not raining now.
 9 Roger **does not** like going to town.
10 The pears **are not** quite ripe.

LONE DOG

I'm a lean dog, a keen dog, a wild dog and lone,
I'm a rough dog, a tough dog, hunting on my own!
I'm a bad dog, a mad dog, teasing silly sheep;
I love to sit and bay at the moon and keep fat souls from sleep.

I'll never be a lap dog, licking dirty feet,
A sleek dog, a meek dog, cringing for my meat.
Not for me the fireside, the well-filled plate,
But shut the door and sharp stone and cuff and kick and hate.

Not for me the other dogs, running by my side,
Some have run a short while, but none of them would bide.
O mine is still the lone trail, the hard trail, the best,
Wide wind and wild stars and the hunger of the quest.

Irene McLeod

(A) Answer these questions.

1 Which word in the first verse rhymes with **lone**?
2 Which word in the first line rhymes with **lean**?
3 Find a pair of words that rhyme in the third line.
4 Make a list of three pairs of words that rhyme in the second verse.
5 Which word in the third verse rhymes with **best**?

(B) How does the dog feel about being a 'lone dog'?

Choose five words from the list below that you think describe his feelings best. (Remember to use a dictionary to check the meanings of the words.)

sad	hungry	defiant
proud	resolute	jealous
lonely	independent	pathetic
happy	bitter	depressed

NOISES OF ANIMALS

I bark

(A) Write the noise words.

1 sheep _____	**5** donkeys _____
2 ducks _____	**6** cockerels _____
3 dogs _____	**7** hens _____
4 cows _____	**8** cats _____

(B) Fill each space with the name of the creature or the name of the noise it makes.

1 The dog was _____ at a squirrel.
2 We heard the cows _____ in the meadow.
3 The loud braying of a _____ frightened the children.
4 The cat was _____ because she had hurt her paw.
5 The _____ bleated as the dog rounded them up.
6 The boys were up before the _____ started crowing.
7 Robert's brown _____ clucked after laying an egg.
8 The _____ quacked as it came towards me.

I crow

I cluck

I bleat

I bray

I quack

I mew

I moo

VERBS

I, you, we, they	he, she, it
do	does
go	goes
put	puts
run	runs
pull	pulls
play	plays
say	says
try	tries
carry	carries
hurry	hurries

I **like** apples.

Sally **likes** apples.

We both **like** apples.

(A) Copy and fill in the missing verb, choosing from the words in bold type.

1 they _____ **go**   goes
2 I _____ **try**   tries
3 he _____ **pull**   pulls
4 you _____ **say**   says
5 we _____ **do**   does
6 she _____ **put**   puts
7 you _____ **hurry**   hurries
8 it _____ **run**   runs
9 I _____ **carry**   carries
10 they _____ **play**   plays

(B) Write the verb from the list on the left that will fill each space correctly.

1 The children _____ football every day.
2 Mr Gold _____ his umbrella on his arm.
3 Judith _____ her knitting by the fire.
4 We _____ to school five days a week.
5 Peter _____ his prayers every night.
6 I will catch the bus if I _____.
7 Our cat always _____ after a mouse.
8 Zena _____ hard to write a good letter.

(C) Write sentences of your own showing how each of these words can be used.

1 make   makes   4 think   thinks
2 eat   eats   5 walk   walks
3 red   reads   6 learn   learns

WRITING LETTERS

(A) Read the letter that Tom Weller wrote to his friend Ben Baxter inviting him to his birthday party. Tom's mother showed him how to arrange the letter and how to address the envelope.

Notice the postcode HD24 3PX. Always show the postcode in the last line of your address.

Pretend you are Ben Baxter and that you have just received this letter from Tom.

Write a letter to him thanking him for his kind invitation and telling him that you will be delighted to come.

Draw an envelope and address it to Tom. You will find his address at the top of his letter.

(B) Pretend that you have been to Tom's party. Write a letter to another friend who was not there, telling him how much you enjoyed yourself. Say what you had to eat, what games you played and what fireworks you saw.

Draw an envelope and address it to your friend.

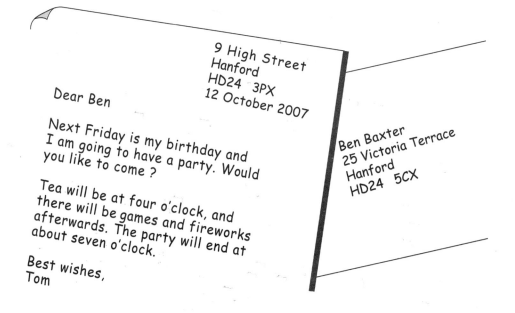

9 High Street
Hanford
HD24 3PX
12 October 2007

Dear Ben

Next Friday is my birthday and I am going to have a party. Would you like to come ?

Tea will be at four o'clock, and there will be games and fireworks afterwards. The party will end at about seven o'clock.

Best wishes,
Tom

Ben Baxter
25 Victoria Terrace
Hanford
HD24 5CX

SOUNDS

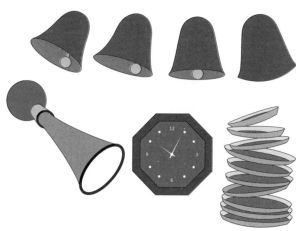

A Write the name of each sound.

1 the _____ of dishes
2 the _____ of a drum
3 the _____ of bells
4 the _____ of a clock
5 the _____ of a door
6 the _____ of a horn
7 the _____ of coins
8 the _____ of raindrops

B Write the **sound** word that suits each sentence.

1 The _____ of raindrops on the window awakened the children.
2 We heard the _____ of drums as the soldiers drew near.
3 The room was so quiet that we could hear the _____ of the clock.
4 I could hear the _____ of coins in his pocket.
5 From the kitchen came the _____ of dishes.
6 With a _____ of the door Jonathan left the room in a bad temper.
7 The car went past with a _____ of the horn.
8 Every Sunday the _____ of church bells could be heard in the village.

COLLECTIVE NOUNS

A number of **sheep** together is called a **flock**.

A number of **tools** together is called a **set**.

Examples

a herd of cows	a pair of shoes	a crowd of people
a litter of puppies	a flight of steps	a pack of wolves
a galaxy of stars	a bunch of grapes	a pack of cards
a flock of sheep	a hand of bananas	a gaggle of geese
a gang of thieves	a suit of clothes	a set of tools
a swarm of bees	a chest of drawers	a host of angels
a shoal of fish		

(A) Write the missing words. You will find them in the list above.

1 a _____ of people
2 a _____ of wolves
3 a _____ of grapes
4 a _____ of shoes
5 a _____ of clothes
6 a flight of _____
7 a chest of _____
8 a shoal of _____
9 a herd of _____
10 a flock of _____

(B) Write the word that will fill each gap.

1 A _____ of steps led to the cabin.
2 A _____ of geese waddled across the yard.
3 Our milk comes from a _____ of Jersey cows.
4 A pack of _____ went hunting in the forest.
5 A _____ of fish swam past our boat.
6 A _____ of people gathered to welcome the Prince.
7 The clothes were kept in an old _____ of drawers.
8 She bought a new _____ of shoes for the wedding.
9 Dad gave his old _____ of clothes to a jumble sale.
10 A _____ of bees settled on Matthew's head and shoulders.

TOM THUMB

The woodman took his family into a very thick wood where they could not see one another ten paces off. The woodman began to cut some wood, and the children to gather up the sticks and to make them into bundles. Their father and mother, seeing them all so busy, crept away from them bit by bit, and then all at once ran away through the bushes.

When the children saw that they had been left alone they started to cry loudly. Tom Thumb let them cry, for he had taken care to drop all along the road the little white stones he had in his pockets.

Then he said to them, "Do not be afraid, brothers. Father and Mother have left us here, but I will take you home again; only follow me."

They followed him, and he brought them home through the wood by the same road as they had come.

Tales from Perrault

1 Where did the woodman take his family?
2 What did he do when they got there?
3 How did the children help their father?
4 What did the father and mother do when the children were busy?
5 Why did the children start to cry?
6 Why did Tom let them cry?
7 What had Tom done on the way to the wood?
8 How was Tom able to take his brothers home again?

GROUP NAMES

The **robin** is a **bird**. So is the **sparrow** and so is the **thrush**.

They all belong to the same **group**. They are all **birds**.

animals	*dogs*	*colours*	*days*	*fish*
flowers	*fruits*	*insects*	*tools*	*trees*

(A) Use a group name from the list above to finish each sentence.

1 Oak, ash, birch and elm are all _____.
2 Terrier, corgi, spaniel and collie are all _____.
3 Hammer, saw, pincers and chisel are all _____.
4 Monday, Thursday, Friday and Tuesday are all _____.
5 Herring, cod, hake and haddock are all _____.
6 Fly, wasp, bee and gnat are all _____.
7 Lion, tiger, bear and wolf are all _____.
8 Red, blue, yellow and green are all _____.
9 Rose, lily, tulip and crocus are all _____.
10 Pear, apple, plum and banana are all _____.

(B) In each column below there is one word that does not belong to the same group as the others.

Write the odd word.

1 willow	**3** blue	**5** apple
oak	bright	orange
birch	black	turnip
daffodil	yellow	lemon
beech	green	pear

2 cow	**4** Christmas	**6** violet
goat	Friday	dandelion
sheep	Wednesday	bluebell
moth	Monday	mushroom
horse	Thursday	snowdrop

PEOPLE WHO WORK

potter	fishmonger
gardener	hairdresser
farmer	flight attendant
teacher	police officer
porter	window cleaner
guard	tennis player
sailor	fire fighter
soldier	

(A) Use the words in the list above to name each person. Number your words 1 to 8 as in the pictures.

(B) Write the missing words. The list above will help you.

1 I asked the _____ when the plane was going to land.
2 The _____ had some fine fillets of hake.
3 The _____ is giving a maths lesson.
4 The _____ wheeled Martin's trunk to the luggage van.
5 Jane has gone to the _____ to have her hair cut.
6 The _____ blew the whistle and the train moved off.
7 The _____ went aboard the battleship.
8 We watched the _____ cutting the hay.
9 The _____ on sentry duty carried a rifle.
10 A big crowd saw the _____ rescue the boy from the burning house.

THE DOERS OF ACTIONS

The person who **teaches** you is your **teacher**.

Teach is the action. **Teacher** is the **doer** of the action.

(A) Add **-er** to each of these verbs to make the name of a doer.

1 help 4 bowl 7 clean
2 build 5 read 8 dream
3 lead 6 paint 9 sing

(B) Before adding **-er** to these words, double the last letter.

1 run 4 win 7 trap
2 rob 5 drum 8 travel
3 shop 6 swim 9 begin

(C) Drop the **e** when you add **-er** to these words.

1 ride 3 drive 5 strike
2 dance 4 explore 6 write

(D) Change **y** to **i** before adding **-er**.

1 carry 2 supply

(E) Write the words that fill the spaces.

1 Sanjay was a strong _____. **swim**
2 The _____ could not keep in step with his partner. **dance**
3 Louise is a very quick _____. **read**
4 The _____ was given a gold medal. **win**
5 He has been a _____ with the band for ten years. **drum**
6 The _____ sent two parcels to the school. **supply**
7 Our _____ keeps the school very tidy. **clean**
8 A policeman stopped the _____ of the sports car. **drive**

MALE AND FEMALE

A **boy** is a **he**, or a **male**. A **man** is a **he**, or a **male**.

A **girl** is a **she**, or a **female**. A **woman** is a **she**, or a **female**.

Male	Female
actor	actress
cockerel	hen
gander	goose
grandfather	grandmother
duke	duchess
prince	princess
son	daughter
tiger	tigress
waiter	waitress
uncle	aunt
nephew	niece
husband	wife
king	queen
ram	ewe
stallion	mare
bull	cow

(A) Copy this column, then write the missing words.

	Male	Female
1	_____	princess
2	grandfather	_____
3	_____	daughter
4	_____	waiter
5	gander	_____
6	_____	queen
7	_____	tigress
8	_____	actress
9	cockerel	_____
10	_____	duchess

(B) Change **male** words to **female**, and **female** to **male**.

1 The waitress took our order and left.
2 The actor tripped over the scenery and fell on his face.
3 The goose hissed at the children.
4 Her husband was at work.
5 The teacher's son was very ill.
6 The hunter shot the huge tiger.
7 The old hen scratched in the earth for worms.
8 In the evening the prince walked in the garden.
9 I gave my nephew £10.
10 My daughter is afraid of cows.

ANIMALS

(A) Write the names of these animals.

(B) Write the name of the animal that will complete each sentence. You will find them in the list on the left.

1 The _____ is covered with sharp spines and can roll itself into a ball when attacked.

2 The _____ has a long trunk and strong tusks.

3 The _____ has a hump on its back and can carry people and goods across the desert.

4 The _____ has a spotted skin and a very long neck.

5 The _____ has a bushy tail that curls over its back.

6 The _____ is a cunning animal that steals chickens.

7 The _____ is called the King of Beasts. Its loud roar frightens many animals.

8 The _____ is a stubborn animal with very long ears. It is sometimes called an ass.

9 The _____ has strong hind legs that enable it to move forward in great leaps.

10 A _____ has a shaggy coat and strong claws. It can hug a person to death.

bear	giraffe
fox	hedgehog
lion	elephant
camel	kangaroo
donkey	squirrel

THE FOX AND THE GOAT

While reaching down to drink the water in a well one day, a fox fell in. Try as he would, he could not get out again because the walls of the well were too high.

Not long after, a goat came along. Seeing the fox down there, he asked him the reason why.

"I am enjoying the cool, pure water," replied the fox. "Wouldn't you like to jump down and taste it?"

Without stopping to think, the foolish old goat jumped down. No sooner had he reached the bottom than the cunning old fox leaped on to his back and scrambled to the top.

Looking down at the unhappy goat, the fox laughed and said, "Next time, friend goat, be sure to look before you leap."

Aesop's Fables

1 What did the fox have to do before he could drink the water in the well?
2 What happened to him while he was doing this?
3 Why could he not get out of the well?
4 What did the goat ask the fox?
5 What was the answer given by the fox?
6 What did the goat do when the fox asked him to try the water?
7 How did the fox get to the top again?
8 What did he tell the goat to do the next time?

ADVERBS

---

*Andrew tiptoed **quietly** from the room.*

The word **quietly** tells us how he left the room.

This word is formed by adding **-ly** to quiet. It is an **adverb**.

(A) Add **-ly** to each of these words.

quick	safe	kind
calm	neat	fond
sad	quiet	proud

(B) When **-ly** is added to words ending with **y**, this letter is first changed to **i**.

Examples   *clumsy*   *hasty*

                   clumsily   *hastily*

Add **-ly** to these words.

easy	lucky	greedy
busy	heavy	hungry
sleepy	angry	weary
noisy	steady	thirsty

(C) The word that fills each space below is formed by adding **-ly** to the word in bold type. Write the nine words.

1 The flames spread so ____ that the house was soon burnt to the ground. **quick**

2 All the boys were working ____. **busy**

3 The ship arrived ____ after a stormy voyage. **safe**

4 The snail crept ____ along the garden path. **slow**

5 The old man nodded his head ____. **sleepy**

6 It is raining too ____ for you to go out. **heavy**

7 The young mother looked ____ at her baby. **proud**

8 Jo wrote the letter very ____. **neat**

9 Zek jumped over the wall quite ____. **easy**

OPPOSITES: CHANGE OF WORDS

Look at this list of opposites, then answer the questions.

back	front	bitter	sweet	poor	rich	noisy	quiet
buy	sell	dark	light	break	mend	fast	slow
		glad	sorry	long	short		

(A) Use the opposite of the word in bold type to fill each space.

Example a fast train **slow**

1 to _____ a rabbit **buy**
2 a _____ room **dark**
3 a _____ seat **back**
4 a _____ story **long**
5 a _____ orange **sweet**
6 a _____ street **quiet**
7 a _____ man **poor**
8 to _____ a toy **break**
9 to be _____ **glad**

(B) Fill each gap with the opposite of the word in bold type.

1 If you _____ your arm it will take about six weeks to **mend**.
2 We are going to paint the **front** and the _____ of our house.
3 He was _____ when his cousin came but **sorry** when he left.
4 Uncle will **sell** his old car and _____ a new one.
5 He tied the _____ length of cord to the **long** one.
6 The children were **quiet** in school but very _____ outside.
7 Ten years ago he was _____. Now he is very **rich**.
8 He wore a **dark** grey suit and a _____ grey hat.
9 The clock was five minutes **fast** yesterday but it is _____ today.

GROUP NAMES

| An apple is a **fruit**. | A cabbage is a **vegetable**. |
| A rose is a **flower**. | A teddy bear is a **toy**. |

| bird | fish | toy | tree | tool |
| fruit | flower | insect | animal | vegetable |

(A) Write the group name for each of these objects. Use the list above to help you.

1 A doll is a ____.
2 A peach is a ____.
3 A herring is a ____.
4 An oak is a ____.
5 A tiger is an ____.

6 A wasp is an ____.
7 A turnip is a ____.
8 A crocus is a ____.
9 A sparrow is a ____.
10 A hammer is a ____.

(B) Draw four columns in your book, like these. Then put the words below in their correct columns.

Fruits	Fishes	Vegetables	Tools

parsnip	cabbage	trowel	plum
rake	lemon	mackerel	salmon
orange	plaice	beetroot	onion
carrot	spade	banana	hatchet
herring	apricot	spanner	hake

(C)

Name a vegetable beginning with **p**.

Name a fruit beginning with **g**.

Name a fish beginning with **s**.

Name a tool beginning with **d**.

FOOD AND DRINK

breakfast	*margarine*	*butter*	*marmalade*
cereals	*milk*	*cream*	*muesli*
eggs	*pudding*	*flour*	*sugar*
juice	*toast*	*kipper*	*wheat*

A Copy these sentences. Use the words in the list above to fill the spaces.

1 Bread, buns and cakes are made from _____.
2 Flour is a fine meal or powder made from _____.
3 Many children have cornflakes, puffed wheat and similar foods for _____.
4 Such foods are known as _____.
5 The _____ we eat are laid by hens.
6 Butter, eggs and sugar are used with rice to make a rice _____.
7 Fruit is boiled with _____ to make jam.
8 Jam made with oranges is called _____.
9 The _____ that we drink comes from the cow.
10 If milk is allowed to stand the _____ rises to the top.
11 The _____ that we spread on our bread is made from milk.
12 Many people eat _____ instead of butter.
13 You make _____ by browning both sides of a slice of bread.
14 The liquid part of fruits and vegetables is called _____.
15 You can make your own _____ by mixing oats, nuts and dried fruit.
16 A _____ is a salted and smoked herring.

ALPHABETICAL ORDER

All these words begin with a different letter.

| **f**ruit | **y**ear | **m**arch | **b**oard | **s**hade |

To put them in **abc** or **alphabetical order** we look at the first letter only.

| **b**oard | **f**ruit | **m**arch | **s**hade | **y**ear |

All these words begin with the same letter.

| **b**ead | **b**lack | **b**rick | **b**ook | **b**ath |

To put them in alphabetical order we must look at the **second** letter in each.

| e | l | r | o | a |

Now it is easy to put them in their right order.

| b**a**th | b**e**ad | b**l**ack | b**o**ok | b**r**ick |

(A) Write the words in each column in alphabetical order.

1 bank	**2** crop	**3** loaf	**4** peck	**5** slot	**6** much
bend	club	lick	part	scar	milk
boat	case	lump	port	ship	meat
bite	chop	lamb	pure	stop	mask
burn	cost	leaf	pine	safe	more

(B) Can you spot the word that is **out of order** in each of these columns?

1 nail	**2** gate	**3** feel	**4** east	**5** pray
nurse	give	from	edge	pill
near	gone	fine	else	plan
nice	glad	flat	echo	post
noon	grow	fuss	even	punt

(C) Put these names in alphabetical order.

John	Joanna	James
Janine	Jeremy	Joseph

THE LION AND THE MOUSE

A lion was asleep in his den one day when a playful little mouse ran up his outstretched paw and across his nose, awakening him from his nap. As quick as lightning the lion clapped his mighty paw upon the frightened little mouse and roared angrily.

"Please don't kill me," squealed the mouse. "Forgive me this time and I will never forget it. One day I may be able to do you a good turn to repay your kindness."

The lion smiled at the mouse, amused by the thought that such a tiny creature would ever be able to help him. So he lifted his paw and let the mouse go.

Later, while the lion was out hunting, he became caught in a net which some men had set to catch him. At once he let out a roar that echoed through the forest. The little mouse heard it, and recognising the voice of the lion who had spared his life, ran to where the king of beasts lay tangled in the net of ropes.

"Well, your majesty," said the mouse, "I know you did not believe me when I said that a day may come when I may repay your kindness, but here is my chance."

At once the little mouse started to nibble through the ropes that bound the lion with his sharp little teeth. Soon the lion was free and able to crawl out of the hunters' snare.

This fable teaches us that no act of kindness, however small, is ever wasted.

Aesop's Fables

1 Which word in the first paragraph means **a short sleep**?
2 How did the mouse wake the lion up?
3 How did the mouse persuade the lion not to kill him?
4 Why was the lion so amused at what the mouse said?
5 What did the men use to catch the lion?
6 How did the mouse recognise the trapped lion?
7 How did the mouse set the lion free?
8 What is the lesson of this fable?
9 Why does the mouse address the
   lion as "your majesty"?

VERBS: PAST TIME

Present time: Past time:
*We **begin** our holidays today.*   *They **began** their holidays yesterday.*

Learn the verbs in this list, then answer the questions.

Present	Past	Present	Past	Present	Past	Present	Past
blow	*blew*	*drive*	*drove*	*fly*	*flew*	*sleep*	*slept*
break	*broke*	*eat*	*ate*	*hide*	*hid*	*take*	*took*
do	*did*	*feel*	*felt*	*know*	*knew*	*tear*	*tore*

(A) Copy these columns. Fill in the blanks.

	Present	Past
1	tear	_____
2	break	_____
3	sleep	_____
4	know	_____
5	_____	took
6	_____	hid
7	_____	drove
8	_____	ate
9	fly	_____
10	_____	blew
11	do	_____
12	_____	felt

(B) Write the verbs in past time that must be used to fill the gaps.

1 Peter _____ a long time to do his sums.
2 Mr Bond _____ the car into the garage.
3 I went to bed early and _____ all night.
4 The high wind _____ the leaves off the trees.
5 Ling _____ a plate when she washed the dishes.
6 The dog _____ all his food and wanted more.
7 The lark _____ up into the sky.
8 James _____ a pain in his side.
9 Martin _____ the answer to every question.
10 Rania _____ her anorak on a rusty nail.

BIRTHDAYS

(A) Read this poem, then answer the questions.

Monday's child is fair of face,
Tuesday's child is full of grace,
Wednesday's child is full of woe,
Thursday's child has far to go,
Friday's child is loving and giving,
Saturday's child works hard for its living,
But the child that is born on a Sunday
Is fair and wise and good and gay.

1 Which child has to work hard for a living?
2 The child born on a Tuesday is full of _____.
3 Which child will be a sad child?
4 Which child will be a pretty child?
5 Which child is loving and giving?
6 What does Thursday's child have to do?
7 What is the child born on a Sunday like?

(B) Write the names of the days of the week in order.

Opposite each day write a sentence about something you do on that day.

Examples

Monday   *I take money to school to pay for my dinners for the week.*

Tuesday   *I borrow a book from the class library.*

Saturday   *I go shopping with my mother.*

HOMOPHONES: SAME SOUND, DIFFERENT MEANING

Some words have the same sound as other words, but they differ in spelling and meaning. They are called **homophones**.

Look at these four pairs of words. Learn to spell each word. Learn the meaning of each.

hear   You **hear** with your ears.
here   I will wait **here** for you.

main   The **main** road is the most important one.
mane   The long hair on the neck of a horse or a lion is called a **mane**.

meat   The flesh of an animal used for food is called **meat**.
meet   When people **meet** they get together.

pail   A **pail** is a kind of bucket.
pale   A **pale** person has little colour.

Choose the correct word from the given pair to complete each sentence.

1 pail   pale
She looked very _____ after her illness.

2 meat   meet
The _____ was too tough to eat.

3 here   hear
We did not _____ the postman knocking.

4 main   mane
The school is on the _____ road.

5 pail   pale
The _____ was half full of water.

6 main   mane
The horse had a very long _____.

7 meat   meet
We will _____ you outside the cinema.

THE MONTHS OF THE YEAR

	January		February		March		April
S	6 13 20 27		3 10 17 24		2 9 16 23 30		6 13 20 27
M	7 14 21 28		4 11 18 25		3 10 17 24 31		7 14 21 28
T	1 8 15 22 29		5 12 19 26		4 11 18 25		1 8 15 22 29
W	2 9 16 23 30		6 13 20 27		5 12 19 26		2 9 16 23 30
Th	3 10 17 24 31		7 14 21 28		6 13 20 27		3 10 17 24
F	4 11 18 25		1 8 15 22 29		7 14 21 28		4 11 18 25
S	5 12 19 26		2 9 16 23		1 8 15 22 29		5 12 19 26

	May		June		July		August
S	4 11 18 25		1 8 15 22 29		6 13 20 27		3 10 17 24 31
M	5 12 19 26		2 9 16 23 30		7 14 21 28		4 11 18 25
T	6 13 20 27		3 10 17 24		1 8 15 22 29		5 12 19 26
W	7 14 21 28		4 11 18 25		2 9 16 23 30		6 13 20 27
Th	1 8 15 22 29		5 12 19 26		3 10 17 24 31		7 14 21 28
F	2 9 16 23 30		6 13 20 27		4 11 18 25		1 8 15 22 29
S	3 10 17 24 31		7 14 21 28		5 12 19 26		2 9 16 23 30

	September		October		November		December
S	7 14 21 28		5 12 19 26		2 9 16 23 30		7 14 21 28
M	1 8 15 22 29		6 13 20 27		3 10 17 24		1 8 15 22 29
T	2 9 16 23 30		7 14 21 28		4 11 18 25		2 9 16 23 30
W	3 10 17 24		1 8 15 22 29		5 12 19 26		3 10 17 24 31
Th	4 11 18 25		2 9 16 23 30		6 13 20 27		4 11 18 25
F	5 12 19 26		3 10 17 24 31		7 14 21 28		5 12 19 26
S	6 13 20 27		4 11 18 25		1 8 15 22 29		6 13 20 27

(A) Look at the calendar. Answer the questions. A year in which February has 29 days is known as a Leap Year.

1 How many months are there in the year?
2 Which month has the shortest name?
3 Write the names of the three months ending with **-ember**.
4 Which month has the longest name?
5 Which month has fewest days?
6 In which month does your birthday come?
7 Name the month in which Christmas comes.
8 Write the names of the four months that have no letter **r** in them.

(B) We can write the names of most of the months in a short way.

Copy these short forms and learn them.

1	January	Jan.	7	July	July
2	February	Feb.	8	August	Aug.
3	March	Mar.	9	September	Sept.
4	April	April	10	October	Oct.
5	May	May	11	November	Nov.
6	June	June	12	December	Dec.

WRITING DATES

Write **st** after the number.

1st   *first*   **21st**   *twenty-first*   **31st**   *thirty-first*

Write **nd** after the number.

2nd   *second*   **22nd**   *twenty-second*

Write **rd** after the number.

3rd   *third*   **23rd**   *twenty-third*

For all other numbers in the calendar add **th**.

4th   *fourth*   **11th**   *eleventh*   **17th**   *seventeenth*
25th   *twenty-fifth*

(A) Use numbers to write these.

1 fifth	**6** third	**11** thirty-first
2 tenth	**7** ninth	**12** seventh
3 second	**8** twenty-first	**13** twenty-third
4 first	**9** sixteenth	**14** twelfth
5 sixth	**10** fourth	**15** twenty-second

(B) Writing dates: 14th May or May 14th

1 Write the date for the twenty-fourth of September.
2 On which date does New Year's Day come?
3 What is the date today?
4 Write the date of your birthday.
5 Write the date for August the twenty-first.
6 On which date does Christmas Day come?

A CAMPING HOLIDAY

Last summer Roger and his sister Jill went on a camping holiday in Wales with their parents for the first time. Their new blue tent, which had two bedrooms and a living-room, was pitched in a large field near a sandy bay. There were no other tents in the field and Roger pretended that they were explorers.

Early every morning the two children and their mother went swimming while their father made the breakfast. When they came back, hungry from their exercise, they found him cooking beans and eggs on a portable gas stove. After breakfast they all went down to the beach and played cricket and enjoyed the sunshine.

In the afternoons the children went fishing with their nets in the clear pools, while their parents sat on the sand reading. In the evening they walked to the farmhouse at the foot of the hill. They watched the cows being milked and then had supper with the farmer and his wife. The farmer told the children all about his animals and his crops and promised to let them help with the harvest if they came back in the autumn. At sunset they strolled back along the deserted road to their tent, climbed into their sleeping bags and fell fast asleep. Nothing disturbed them until the singing of the birds woke them next morning.

True or false?
Write in your book the statements
that are true.

1 Roger and Jill had not been camping before.
2 Their father cooked the supper every evening.
3 The camp site was very crowded.
4 The children slept soundly at night.
5 **Portable** means 'easily carried'.
6 The beach was quite close.
7 The family got up early every morning.
8 They all went fishing in the afternoons.

RHYMES

car	star	bar	tar
far	jar	are	bar
lie	high	shy	high
sly	pie	sky	sty
let	set	bet	net
pet	met	wet	yet
tight	fight	sight	light
right	night	might	white

(A) Read this poem carefully. Then copy it, putting in the words that you think will end each line.

Twinkle, twinkle, little _____.
How I wonder what you _____!
Up above the world so _____
Like a diamond in the _____.

When the blazing sun is _____,
And the grass with dew is _____,
Then you show your little _____.
Twinkle, twinkle, all the _____.

(B) Write the list of words in capital letters. After each word write the three words in small letters that will rhyme with it.

Example **1** *LATE* gate, weight, wait

1 LATE   mend   park   stout
2 BARK   gate   pout   sing
3 OUT   cling   weight   lend
4 BEND   mark   about   bring
5 RING   wait   lark   send

(C) The missing word in each line below rhymes with the word in bold type.

1 Two pence is a _____ sum of money.   **crawl**
2 I will _____ you at the corner of the street.   **heat**
3 The bread was too _____ to eat.   **nail**
4 If you _____ a dog he may bite you.   **keys**
5 Mum asked Sally to _____ the tea.   **snore**

COMPOUND WORDS

> A **compound** word is formed by joining together two or more words.
>
> *Example*   tea + pot = ***teapot***
>
> | | | | |
> |---|---|---|---|
> | *armchair* | *butterfly* | *hedgehog* | *broomstick* |
> | *wheelbarrow* | *silkworm* | *snowdrop* | *blackboard* |
> | *birdcage* | *cowboy* | *dustbin* | |
> | *matchbox* | *bulldog* | *greenhouse* | |

(A) How many things can you see in the picture whose names are compound words? The list above the picture may help you. Write the name of each object. Show the two words that make up each compound word.

Example   rail + way = ***railway***

(B) In each line below, join together the two words in bold type to form a compound word. Start with the second word.

1 a **fish** that is **gold** in colour
2 a **boat** that is driven by a **motor**
3 a **shade** over a **lamp**
4 a **cloth** that covers a **table**
5 a **ball** made of **snow**
6 a **room** for a **bed**
7 **weed** that grows in the **sea**
8 a **tray** to hold cigarette **ash**
9 a **box** for keeping **cash**

THE LONG AND THE SHORT

There is a short way of writing some words. They are called **abbreviations**. Some have a full stop after them, but not all of them do.

Avenue	*Ave.*	*Mister*	*Mr*	*Street*	*St.*
Doctor	*Dr*	*Road*	*Rd*	*Terrace*	*Ter.*
Mistress	*Mrs*	*Square*	*Sq.*		

Initials

Instead of writing a person's first names in full we write only the **first letter**, as a **capital**, followed by a full stop.

Edward Marsh	*Arthur John Bond*	*Joanna Long*
E. Marsh	*A. J. Bond*	*J. Long*

(A) Write each of these the short way:

1 Doctor Smith	**3** Mister Lee	**5** Mistress Bond	**7** Victoria Square
2 High Street	**4** Station Terrace	**6** Bush Avenue	**8** Redlands Road

(B) Draw envelopes in your exercise book and write these names and addresses, using initials and the short forms you have learnt.

1 Mister Ronald Green, of 12 Church Street, Camford, CP20 3NF.

2 Mistress Jane Everson, of 9 Norton Road, Benham, BP13 4QT.

3 Miss Eva May Brent, of 16 Park Terrace, Broxley, BI58 2RV.

4 Doctor Ann June Johnson, of 25 Poplar Avenue, Reddington, RN41 9GH.

5 Mister Sanjay Prasad, of 31 Chester Square, Podworth, PE57 9AL.

SHORT FORMS

The short way of writing **has not** is **hasn't**.

We can also write **that is** a short way – **that's**.

In a similar way the word **will** can be added to words and written in a short way.

| I will | I'll | he will | he'll | we will | we'll |
| you will | you'll | she will | she'll | they will | they'll |

Remember that the **'** shows that the letters **wi** have been left out.

(A) Write the short form for:

1 is not   6 do not   11 I will
2 we will   7 where is   12 does not
3 here is   8 you will   13 it is
4 he will   9 did not   14 she will
5 are not   10 they will   15 what is

(B) Write the short form of the two words in bold type in these sentences.

1 I know **you will** be pleased with your present.
2 Nishani says **there is** plenty of time.
3 Next time **we will** go by train.
4 We must find out **who is** going to the party.
5 I promise you **I will** do my best.
6 If Melanie is late **she will** be scolded.
7 The boys say **they will** call on their way home.
8 Aled **would not** get up when called.
9 It is very likely **he will** be late for school.
10 Everybody says **it is** a fine drawing.

(C) Change these short forms back into two words.

1 haven't   6 couldn't
2 he'll   7 it's
3 don't   8 she'll
4 she's   9 shouldn't
5 didn't   10 wasn't

SYNONYMS

a **plucky** sailor

a **brave** sailor

The words **plucky** and **brave** are similar in meaning. They are called **synonyms**.

Learn the list of synonyms, then answer the questions.

aged	old	cash	money
connect	join	garments	clothes
glance	look	handsome	beautiful
loiter	linger	plump	fat
slender	slim	tremble	shake

Ⓐ For each word in bold type give a word that has a similar meaning.

1 The **cash** was taken to the bank.
2 The plumber came to **connect** the pipes.
3 He is a very **handsome** child.
4 The Browns had a **plump** turkey for Christmas.
5 You should not **loiter** on the way home.
6 He did not even **glance** at the book.
7 The dancer has a **slender** figure.
8 The door was opened by an **aged** man.
9 The trains made the old bridge **tremble**.
10 All **garments** sold in this shop are tailor made.

Ⓑ Write simpler words that are similar in meaning to these. Some you have already learnt in Book 1.

1 broad	5 repair	9 commence	13 correct
2 plucky	6 collect	10 reply	14 peril
3 finish	7 difficult	11 wealthy	15 assist
4 large	8 stout	12 weeping	16 farewell

ANDROCLES AND THE LION

Once, long ago, a shepherd was roaming the hot, desert land of Africa when he met a lion. He was very frightened, but when he saw that the lion had a thorn in its paw and was in terrible pain he walked towards it, spoke to it gently and pulled out the thorn. From that time on, Androcles and the lion were great friends.

Some time later some soldiers came and arrested Androcles. They took him far across the sea to the great city of Rome. The Emperor of Rome tried to make Androcles give up his Christian faith, and when he refused had him thrown into a huge arena to be torn apart and eaten by a fierce lion.

Androcles saw the lion spring towards him. Then, suddenly, the lion stopped, bowed its head and held out its paw. Androcles knew then that this lion was his friend from the desert of Africa who had been captured by hunters and brought to Rome.

The Emperor was amazed. "You and your lion have been loyal and brave, Androcles," he said. "You shall both be released at once."

So Androcles and the lion returned across the sea to their home in the desert land of Africa.

1 Where did Androcles first meet the lion?
2 What work did Androcles do for his living?
3 How did Androcles feel when he first saw the lion?
4 What does **arrested** mean?
5 How do you know the Emperor of Rome was not a Christian?
6 How did the Emperor plan to punish Androcles?
7 Why did the Emperor release Androcles and the lion?
8 Where did they go when they were released?
9 Androcles was loyal and brave. Write a sentence to say what else you think he was, and why you think this.

FUN WITH WORDS

In each group of words below are two pairs of words and one odd word.

You have to find the word that will make up the third pair.

Look at the first pair of words: *ten   tent*

The second word is made by writing the letter **t** after the first word.

Look at the second pair. The second word is again formed by writing **t** after the first word: *sea   seat*

To find the missing word write **t** after the odd word, *star*.

Example   star   start

(A) Now find the other missing words. In each group a different letter must be added.

1 ten   tent   **3** pan   pane   **5** bun   bung
    sea   seat   hop   hope   ran   rang
    star   hid   thin

2 ten   tend   **4** tea   team
    ban   band   for   form
    win   war

(B) From the letters in the word **tens** we can make the word **nest**.

From the letters in the words in bold type make words that will fit into the spaces below.

1 There were five eggs in the _____.   **tens**
2 The smallest pony was quite _____.   **meat**
3 The journey was a very _____ one.   **owls**
4 Every child should learn to _____ well.   **dare**
5 We should take great _____ with our spelling.   **race**

MORE FUN WITH WORDS

(A) Each dash in these sentences stands for a letter. Each group of letters spells a word.

Example

Mary has long g _ _ _ en hair.
*The missing letters are **old**.*

Each missing word has **three** letters. Write the missing words only.

1 The plants were bl _ _ _ down by the strong wind.
2 The little boy sat down on the three-legged S _ _ _ l.
3 We sometimes have snow in the _ _ _ ter.
4 Wolves were h _ _ _ ing in the forest.
5 The _ _ _ tain of the ship was a Dane.
6 The mon _ _ _ hung from the tree by his long tail.

(B) Each missing word has **four** letters. Write the missing words only.

1 Wendy's class will have a new t _ _ _ _ er next term.
2 Bees had s _ _ _ _ ed on an apple tree in the garden.
3 The tired horse was taken to the st _ _ _ _ _.
4 Mum turned on the heater because the room was c _ _ _ _ y.
5 The engine was letting off s _ _ _ _.
6 We saw the p _ _ _ _ landing on the runway.
7 The express t _ _ _ _ ran off the rails.

VERBS: PAST TIME

Present time:
*I **feel** a pain in my side today.*

Past time:
*I **felt** a pain in my side yesterday.*

Learn the words in this list, then answer the questions.

Present	Past	Present	Past
build	built	rise	rose
creep	crept	see	saw
grow	grew	sink	sank
ride	rode	speak	spoke
ring	rang	steal	stole

(A) Copy these columns. Fill in the blanks.

	Present	Past		Present	Past
1	_____	saw	6	speak	_____
2	_____	rang	7	steal	_____
3	_____	rose	8	ride	_____
4	_____	grew	9	build	_____
5	_____	sank	10	creep	_____

(B) Write the verbs in past time that will fill the gaps.

1 He _____ to the seaside on his new bicycle.
2 The boat filled with water and _____.
3 The boy _____ the school bell.
4 The gardener _____ some beautiful roses.
5 I _____ to him on the telephone.
6 The boys _____ a sandcastle on the beach.
7 We _____ two bear cubs in the zoo.
8 The thief _____ the money from the till.
9 The sun _____ at six o'clock yesterday morning.
10 The burglar _____ quietly into the house.

USING *TOOK* AND *TAKEN*

I **took** a book home.

I **have taken** a book home. (**have** helps the word **taken**)

The book **was taken** home. (**was** helps the word **taken**)

The word **took** needs no helping word.

The word **taken** always has a helping word:

is taken	*are taken*	*has taken*	*had taken*
was taken	*were taken*	*have taken*	*will be taken*

(A) Use **took** or **taken** to fill each space.

1 It was _____   6 You have _____
2 You _____   7 He _____
3 He has _____   8 We were _____
4 I _____   9 It will be _____
5 They are _____   10 She _____

(B) Fill each space with **took** or **taken**.

1 The man was _____ ill at the football match.
2 They _____ the man to the hospital.
3 Bela _____ her cocoa to bed with her.
4 She _____ two pills after dinner.
5 The thief _____ all the money in the house.
6 Carly has _____ great care with her work.
7 The two men were _____ to prison.
8 After Alan had _____ his shoes to the shoe repairer he went fishing.
9 As it was raining Ramu _____ his umbrella.
10 The dustmen have _____ the rubbish away.

WHEN PEOPLE SPEAK

Look at this sentence:

"This orange is sour," said Robert.

The words spoken by Robert were

This orange is sour.

Notice the speech marks come before the first word spoken "**This** . . . and after the last word spoken . . . **sour**,". Notice that the speech marks come after the comma: . . . **sour**,".

The speech marks would also come after a question mark:

"Is the orange sour?" asked Robert.

(A) Copy these sentences. Put in the speech marks.

  1 Pass me the sugar, please, said Mrs Sandhu.
  2 Are you tired? asked the teacher.
  3 I can see you, shouted Ben.
  4 Please, Mummy, may I have an apple? begged Simon.
  5 Come here, Spot, said the little boy to his dog.
  6 I don't want to go to bed yet, said Sandra with a pout.
  7 Hurry up, Lila, or you'll be late, said her mother.
  8 Spare a penny for the guy, please? asked the two boys.
  9 Here is fifty pence for you, replied the man.
10 Be quiet, baby's sleeping, whispered Jemma's mother.

(B) Write three sentences of your own in which there are words spoken by people.

JOHN AND THE CHERRIES

One day John went shopping with his mother. Their first call was at the greengrocer's, and while his mother was buying some fruit John looked longingly at a box containing lovely red cherries.

"Help yourself to a handful, John," said the greengrocer, but John did not move.

"I'm sure you like cherries, don't you?" asked the puzzled shopkeeper, and John nodded his head quickly. Thinking that the boy was too shy to help himself, the greengrocer went to the box and gave John a large handful.

When they had left the shop John's mother asked him why he had not taken the cherries when the greengrocer had told him to.

"Well, you see, Mummy," replied John, "his hand is twice as big as mine."

1 At what shop did John and his mother call first?
2 Explain what looking **longingly** means.
3 What did the greengrocer tell John to do?
4 Did John do as he was told?
5 What did the greengrocer do when he saw John was so shy?
6 Which word describes John best? Why?

    clever   **greedy**
    rude   **cunning**

WRITE THE MISSING WORDS

(A) **1** A sheep is covered with _____.
      A rabbit is covered with _____.

 2 A young cat is called a _____.
      A young dog is called a _____.

 3 A dog barks.
      A lion _____.

 4 The meat from a cow is called _____.
      The meat from a sheep is called _____.

 5 A bus travels on land.
      A ship travels on _____.

 6 Mr is a short way of writing Mister.
      Dr is a short way of writing _____.

 7 You see with your eyes.
      You smell with your _____.

 8 Your foot is at the end of your _____.
      Your hand is at the end of your _____.

(B) We can put these pairs of statements in a different way.

For the first pair we can write:

***Sheep** is to **wool** as rabbit is to <u>fur</u>.*

Now write the missing words.

 1 **Cat** is to **kitten** as **dog** is to _____.
 2 **Dog** is to **bark** as **lion** is to _____.
 3 **Cow** is to **beef** as **sheep** is to _____.
 4 **Ship** is to **sea** as **bus** is to _____.
 5 **Mr** is to **Mister** as **Dr** is to _____.
 6 **See** is to **eyes** as **smell** is to _____.

COMPOUND WORDS

A **compound word** is made up of two or more words:
tooth + *brush* = ***toothbrush***

Examples   *cowboy*   *lighthouse*   *snowdrop*   *matchbox*

(A) Write the names of four objects in the picture whose names are compound words. Show the two words from which each has been built up.

(B) In each line join the two words in bold type, beginning with the second of them.

Example   **1**   *sunlight*

1 the **light** given by the **sun**
2 **paper** that is stuck on a **wall** of a room
3 the **teacher** who is **head** of a school
4 part of a bike to **guard** cyclists from **mud**
5 the **pole** to which a **flag** is attached
6 the **stick** to which a **broom** is fastened
7 the **yard** outside a **farm**
8 a **dress** worn by girls and women at **night**
9 a **room** for a **class** of children

JOINING SENTENCES USING CONJUNCTIONS

Paul closed his book.
He put it away.   (two sentences)

*Paul closed his book **and** put it away.*   (one sentence)

The word **and** joins the two sentences.

A word that joins two groups of words or two sentences is called a **conjunction**.

and	for	because	before	if	where
but	as	while	after	whether	although
or	since	when	until	unless	

(A) Join each pair of sentences below, using a suitable conjunction from the list above.

1 The boy got out of bed.
He stretched his arms.

2 We intended to swim.
The water was too cold.

3 We went to bed early.
We were so tired.

4 The children made their way home.
It was getting dark.

5 Ben made some tea.
His mother bathed the baby.

6 Do your homework.
Have your tea.

7 She was very unpopular.
She was so sarcastic.

8 You can do it yourself.
You are so clever.

(B) Write a suitable conjunction in each space.

1 Would you like a cup of tea _____ would you prefer coffee?

2 There will be more accidents at the crossroads _____ a roundabout is built there soon.

3 _____ it poured with rain all day, everyone enjoyed the outing.

4 I enjoyed the film _____ I had seen it before.

5 We intend to go _____ it snows or not.

6 Please do nothing _____ you hear from me.

7 The pupils visited St Paul's Cathedral _____ they were shown the Whispering Gallery.

70

USING THE RIGHT VERB

bandage	drive	learn	play	row
catch	fight	plant	roast	strike

(A) Write the verb from the list above that fits each space.

1 to _____ a boat   **6** to _____ a cold
2 to _____ meat   **7** to _____ a game
3 to _____ a car   **8** to _____ a battle
4 to _____ a tree   **9** to _____ a cut
5 to _____ a lesson   **10** to _____ a blow

built	wrapped	sheltered	stamped	thanked
mounted	returned	spent	taught	warmed

(B) Choose the right word from the list above to finish each sentence.

1 We _____ from the rain in an old barn.
2 James _____ from his holiday yesterday.
3 The carol singers _____ their feet to get warm.
4 Dad _____ me to ride a bicycle.
5 Mel has _____ all her money.
6 I _____ the present and gave it to Kai.
7 Maria _____ herself by the blazing fire.
8 The new house was _____ in less than six months.
9 I _____ my aunt for the money she sent me.
10 The cowboy _____ his horse and rode off.

(C) Use each pair of words in a sentence of your own.

1 bought   sweets   **4** burnt   toast
2 sang   carol   **5** drank   tea
3 posted   letter   **6** rang   bell

WHERE THEY LIVE

| den | web | cage | hutch | kennel |
| sty | nest | hive | shell | stable |

(A) Copy these sentences, filling each space with the name of the home of each creature. You can choose from the list of names above.

1 A snail carries its home, a _____, on its back.
2 The old sow and her piglets were lying down in their _____.
3 Martin made a cosy _____ for his pet rabbit.
4 The lion was in his _____ playing with his cubs.
5 Black Beauty was put in a _____ with another horse.
6 A swarm of bees flew out of the _____.
7 We watched the spider weaving its _____.
8 There are now two budgerigars in the _____.
9 The little terrier was fast asleep in his _____.
10 There were five eggs in the robin's _____.

(B) Use your dictionary to find out who lives in these places.

1 a monastery
2 a barracks
3 a cell
4 a convent
5 a palace

BLACK BEAUTY AND GINGER

My master and mistress made up their minds to pay a visit to some friends who lived about forty-six miles from our home. James was to drive them in the carriage, which was to be drawn by Ginger and me.

The first day we travelled thirty-two miles. There were some long, steep hills, but James drove so carefully that we were never tired or troubled. He never forgot to put on the brake as we went downhill, nor to take it off at the right place. He kept our feet on the smoothest part of the road; and if the uphill was very long he set the wheels a little across the road, so that the carriage should not run back, and gave us time to breathe. All these little things, together with kind words, help a horse very much.

We stopped once or twice on the road; and just as the sun was going down, we reached the town where we were to spend the night. We stopped at the biggest hotel, which was in the Market Place. We drove under an archway into a long yard, at the end of which were the stables where we were to rest.

From *Black Beauty* by Anna Sewell

1 What did Black Beauty's master and mistress make up their minds to do?
2 How far did they travel the first day?
3 Why were the horses never tired or troubled?
4 What did James do as they went downhill?
5 Why did James set the carriage wheels across the road when going up a long hill?
6 At what time of day did they reach the town?
7 Where did they stop?
8 Where were the stables in which the two horses were to spend the night?

USING *ATE* AND *EATEN*

> *George* **ate** *his apple.*
> *George* **has eaten** *his apple.* (**has** helps the word **eaten**)
>
> *The apple* **was eaten** *by George.* (**was** helps the word **eaten**)
>
> The word **ate** needs no helping word.
>
> The word **eaten** always has a helping word:
>
> | | | | |
> |---|---|---|---|
> | *has eaten* | *is eaten* | *was eaten* | *had eaten* |
> | *have eaten* | *are eaten* | *were eaten* | |

(A) Use **ate** or **eaten** to fill each space.

1 I _____
2 You have _____
3 It was _____
4 He _____
5 You _____

6 He has _____
7 We _____
8 They _____
9 She _____
10 We had _____

(B) Fill each space with **ate** or **eaten**.

1 John _____ his supper and went to bed.
2 After John had _____ his supper he went to bed.
3 Many meals are _____ on the beach in summer.
4 The monkey _____ all the nuts the children gave him.
5 The sweater was _____ by moths.
6 The little bear's porridge had been _____ by Goldilocks.
7 The puppy _____ his food and looked for more.
8 When you have _____ your food you may leave the table.
9 Esam _____ the icing and left the cake.
10 Bread is _____ all over the world.

(C) Complete these sentences.

1 Eat ....
2 .... has eaten ....?
3 .... ate ....

RHYMES

mouse	eyes	day	hall	quays	noon
house	rise	way	wall	trees	moon

The last word has been left out of each line in this poem. You will find these rhyming words in the list above.

(A) Copy the poem, filling in the missing words.

The moon

The moon has a face like the clock in the _____;
She shines on thieves on the garden _____,
On streets and fields and harbour _____,
And birds asleep in the forks of _____.

The squalling cat and the squeaking _____,
The howling dog by the door of the _____,
The bat that lies in bed at _____,
All love to be out by the light of the _____.

But all of the things that belong to the _____
Cuddle to sleep to be out of her _____;
And flowers and children close their _____
Till up in the morning the sun shall _____.

(B) In each group below write three other words that rhyme with the word in bold type. The first letters are given to help you.

1 bat	**2 lard**	**3 tack**
r _ _	c _ _ _	r _ _ _
h _ _	y _ _ _	bl _ _ _
p _ _	h _ _ _	st _ _ _

4 and	**5 bag**	**6 lick**
h _ _ _	fl _ _	p _ _ _
br _ _ _	dr _ _	tr _ _ _
gr _ _ _	st _ _	qu _ _ _

SENTENCES

(A) Write the beginning of each sentence. Then choose the ending that will match it.

Example   **1**   *The greedy boy was ill because he had eaten too much.*

Beginning	**Ending**
1 The greedy boy was ill	Simon looked hot and tired.
2 It was raining so heavily	the ship of the desert.
3 As Robert was covered with spots	in a dozen.
4 After mowing the lawn	please let me know.
5 The camel is often called	and went off to school.
6 The load carried by a ship	that the ponds were frozen.
7 Paul picked up his satchel	because he had eaten too much.
8 If you want any help	his mother sent for the doctor.
9 The weather was so cold	is called a cargo.
10 There are twelve things	that Brian put on his mackintosh.

(B) Copy these beginnings. Add your own endings.

1 Roger burst into tears…
2 Just as I left the house…
3 Every summer…
4 Although he is intelligent…

(C) Begin each sentence in your own way.

1 .... a very long way from home.
2 .... and we were soaking wet.
3 .... because he felt so tired.
4 .... and everyone laughed.

FORMING ADJECTIVES

Many adjectives are formed by adding **-ful** to a noun.

Examples

hope + full = hope**ful** (full of hope)
joy + full = joy**ful** (full of joy)

Note that when adding **-full** one **l** is dropped.

beauti**ful**	harm**ful**	pain**ful**	play**ful**	truth**ful**
care**ful**	help**ful**	peace**ful**	thank**ful**	use**ful**

(A) Choose from the list above the adjective ending with **-ful** that will fill each gap.

1 a kitten that is full of play   a _____ kitten
2 a village in which there is peace   a _____ village
3 a girl of great beauty   a _____ girl
4 a driver who takes great care   a _____ driver
5 a cut that gives much pain   a _____ cut
6 a book that is of great use   a _____ book
7 a friend who gives help   a _____ friend
8 a person who is full of thanks   a _____ person
9 a boy who speaks the truth   a _____ boy
10 a habit that causes harm   a _____ habit

(B) Add **-ful** to each of these words. Then choose three of the words you have made and use them in sentences of your own; one word in each sentence.

1 shame   **4** cheer   **7** disgrace
2 delight   **5** hope   **8** boast
3 wonder   **6** hate   **9** rest

OPPOSITES: CHANGE OF WORDS

Learn the list of **opposites**, then answer the questions.

always	never	evil	good
asleep	awake	heavy	light
better	worse	less	more
blunt	sharp	narrow	wide
cruel	kind	pull	push

(A) Use the **opposite** of the word in bold type to fill each space.

Example   **1**   a <u>short</u> story   **long**

1 a _____ knife   **sharp**
2 a _____ master   **kind**
3 he was _____   **asleep**
4 _____ danger   **more**
5 a _____ road   **narrow**
6 a _____ parcel   **light**
7 to _____ the door   **push**
8 _____ tired   **always**
9 a _____ player   **better**

(B) You need opposites again here to fill the spaces.

1 That exercise was **easy** but this one is _____.

2 I am always **polite** but you are very _____.

3 This is the **cold** tap and that is the _____ one.

4 Your face is **clean** but your hands are _____.

5 My uncle is very **generous** but my aunt is _____.

6 As the postman **departed** the window-cleaner _____.

7 Twenty pupils were **present** and only one pupil was _____.

8 This road is **dangerous** but that one is _____.

9 You are **rich** and I am _____.

10 The answer is either **right** or _____.

FEEDING THE CATS

"I'll give this gravy to the cats,"
I heard my mother say in the dark outside the kitchen door;
but the gravy went astray; the scrubbing brush she spilt it on
got up and walked away.

"I hope it's got some friends," Mum said,
"or perhaps some babies, who
can get their tongues between the prickles –
a tricky thing to do.
In future when I feed the cats
I'll feed the hedgehogs too."

Fleur Adcock

Copy and complete these sentences.

1 The mother went into the garden to give the gravy to the _____.
2 The **scrubbing brush** that walked away was really a _____.
3 **Tricky** in verse two means _____.
4 Three words that rhyme in the first verse are _____, _____ and _____.
5 Three words that rhyme in the second verse are _____, _____ and _____.
6 The title of the poem is _____.
7 It was written by _____.

HOMOPHONES: SAME SOUND, DIFFERENT MEANING

Some words have the same sound as other words, but they differ in spelling and meaning. We call them **homophones**.

Look at these four pairs of words. Learn to spell each word. Learn the meaning of each.

pain   *He felt no pain when he had his tooth out.*
pane   *A new **pane** of glass was fixed in the window.*

road   *Many cars were parked at the side of the **road**.*
rode   *Ian **rode** to school on his new bicycle.*

sail   *One **sail** of the ship was torn by the strong wind.*
sale   *All goods were very cheap at the **sale**.*

there *I left the dish **there**. (in that place)*
their *The two boys had lost **their** pencils. (belonging to them)*

Choose the correct word from the pair in bold type to complete each sentence.

1 road   rode
The _____ was muddy after the heavy rain.
2 sail   sale
Helen bought the carpet at a _____.
3 pain   pane
Susan had a _____ in her arm.
4 road   rode
Alan _____ his pony over the fields.
5 there   their
We waited _____ for an hour.
6 pain   pane
The cricket ball broke a _____ in the window.
7 sail   sale
The _____ of the yacht was lowered as it reached the shore.

CONTAINERS

A **purse** holds or contains **money**.

A **jug** contains **water**.

Both are called **containers**.

bin	*cup*	*basket*
jug	*purse*	*teapot*
vase	*suitcase*	*envelope*

(A) Copy the sentences. Write the name of a container in each space.

1 Marion had no loose change in her _____.
2 The _____ was full of rubbish.
3 I drink a _____ of tea at eleven o'clock every morning.
4 There was no milk left in the _____.
5 Pack your clothes in this _____.
6 Some people carry their shopping in a _____.
7 David put the letter in the _____ and posted it.
8 There were some beautiful tulips in the _____.

(B) What would these containers contain? Use your dictionary to find out.

1 decanter
2 scabbard
3 portfolio
4 carafe

25 Victoria Terrace
Hanford HD24 5CX

Tom Weller
1 High Street
Hanford
HD24 3PX

USING LONGER WORDS

The word **where** can be joined to **any**, **every**, **no** and **some**.

*any + where = **anywhere***   *no + where = **nowhere***
*every + where = **everywhere***   *some + where = **somewhere***

The word **body** can be joined to **any**, **every**, **no** and **some**.

*any + body = **anybody***   *no + body = **nobody***
*every + body = **everybody***   *some + body = **somebody***

The word **ever** can be joined to **when**, **where**, **who**, **what**, **how** and **which**.

whenever   *whoever*   *however*
wherever   *whatever*   *whichever*

(A) Use one of these longer words to fill each space.

 1 The hammer must be _____ in the house.
 2 We looked _____ for the lost hammer.
 3 The hammer was _____ to be seen.
 4 We could not find the hammer _____.

(B) Write the words that will fill the gaps.

 1 I don't think there is _____ at home.
 2 We should be kind to _____.
 3 You must get _____ to help you in the garden.
 4 Jake knocked at the door but _____ answered.

(C) Write the **-ever** words that will finish these
sentences.

 1 He never wears a hat _____ cold the weather is.
 2 People must buy food _____ it costs.
 3 _____ took the money must give it back.
 4 You can visit us _____ you like.
 5 Jason's dog follows him _____ he goes.
 6 Take _____ of the two cakes you want.

COMPOUND WORDS USING HYPHENS

You know that compound words are formed by joining together two or more words (**tea** + **pot** = **teapot**).

Some compound words need hyphens.

twenty + *eight* = ***twenty-eight***
walkie + *talkie* = ***walkie-talkie***
happy + *go* + *lucky* = ***happy-go-lucky***

(A) Join these words together with a hyphen.

    1 upside + down
    2 stepping + stone
    3 forty + six
    4 heavy + duty
    5 right + handed

(B) Join each pair of words below to form a compound word. Decide which ones need hyphens. If you are not sure, check in a dictionary.

1 horse + box	**6** old + fashioned	**11** skate + board
2 clock + work	**7** life + boat	**12** kick + off
3 left + handed	**8** roller + skate	**13** high + pitched
4 step + mother	**9** day + dream	**14** machine + gun
5 hand + kerchief	**10** spot + light	**15** make + up

HOMONYMS: WORDS WITH MORE THAN ONE MEANING

Some words have more than one meaning.

*We went to visit an old tin **mine** in Cornwall.*

*The red towel is **mine** but the blue one belongs to Sally.*

blind	foot	mean	rock	top
felt	long	ring	suit	trunk

(A) Use the words in the list above to fill these spaces. The same word must be used for each pair of sentences.

1 The dress is too _____ so I must shorten it.
   I often _____ for a holiday in Spain.
2 The miser was too _____ to buy food for himself.
   Some words _____ much the same as other words.
3 I think this dress will _____ you.
   Henry wore a navy blue _____ at the wedding.
4 Under the carpet was a layer of _____.
   Kamal _____ ill, so she went to bed early.
5 A _____ person cannot see.
   She pulled the _____ down over the window.
6 Mum packed the _____ for the holidays.
   The elephant took the bun with his long _____.
7 There was a hostel at the _____ of the mountain.
   He was lame because he had hurt his _____.
8 Please _____ the doorbell.
   Neeta wore a _____ on each finger.
9 On the beach was a huge _____.
   Jane tried to _____ the baby to sleep.
10 Humpty Dumpty was sitting on _____ of
   the wall. The red _____ was spinning
   round and round.

(B) Make up sentences to show that each of
these words has two meanings.

1 box
2 letter
3 wood
4 stick
5 match

A BEAR CUB'S ADVENTURE

Bears have an excellent sense of smell, and very keen hearing... and scent the faintest odour from a great distance. This is fortunate for them, as they are very short-sighted.

A breeze arose, wafting the odour of something sweet towards Mishook the bear cub. What could it be? The cub did not know, but his mother and the elder ones recognised the aroma of honey ...

With hurried steps the whole bear family set off in search of the prize. They trotted along for about a kilometre before they reached the old decayed tree-trunk where the bees had taken up their abode. The poor bees saw the plunderers, and immediately sounded an alarm. They then defended their store of honey ... by fiercely stinging the bears.

But the mother bear and her cubs ... calmly continued their feast of honey, their thick fur protecting them against the attacks of the bees. One angry bee, however, plunged its sting into Mishook's nose. He growled furiously, shook his head, jumped, snorted, turned round like a spinning-top, and it was with great difficulty that he managed to beat off the troublesome insect with his paws. But this repulse did not by any means prevent him from tasting his share of the honey, of which he immediately became very fond.

From *Baby Mishook* by Leon Golschmann

1 Bears have two senses that are better developed than the others. What are they?
2 Why are the bears fortunate in having these senses?
3 What was the odour that the breeze blew towards Mishook?
4 Where had the bees made their nest?
5 What does **sounded an alarm** mean?
6 How did the bees defend their store of honey?
7 Why were the bears able to continue their feast of honey?
8 Which of the bear family was stung by an angry bee?
9 The bear tried to get rid of the bee by doing six different things. Which one was successful?

THE MEANING OF PREFIXES *mono-, bi-, tri-*

A **prefix** is a syllable or syllables joined to the **beginning** of a word.

Understanding the meaning of the prefix helps you understand the meaning of the word.

mono- means ONE

Example **Monoplane** – *an aeroplane with* **one** *pair of wings.*

bi- means TWO

Example **Bicycle** – *a cycle with* **two** *wheels.*

tri- means THREE

Example **Tripod** – *a stand with* **three** *legs.*

Use your dictionary to find out the meaning of the prefixes in these words.

(A) 1 What kind of word is a monosyllable?
  2 What kind of voice is monotonous?
  3 What kind of railway is a monorail?
  4 What kind of monument is a monolith?

(B) 1 A biped has two _____.
  2 A bivalve has two _____.
  3 To bisect is to cut into two _____.
  4 Binoculars have two _____.

(C) 1 A triangle has three _____.
  2 A tricycle has three _____.
  3 Triennial means happening every three _____.
  4 A trireme is a galley (ship) with three _____.

(D) What is the meaning of these words?

  1 bilingual   4 monogram
  2 triplets   5 trident
  3 biplane

USING *GAVE* AND *GIVEN*

Aunt Judy **gave** Paul fifty pence.
Aunt Judy **has given** Paul fifty pence.
(**has** helps the word **given**)

Paul **was given** fifty pence by Aunt Judy.
(**was** helps the word **given**)

The word **gave** needs no helping word.

The word **given** always has a helping word:

has given	is given	was given	had given
have given	are given	were given	

(A) Use **gave** and **given** to fill each space.

1 He has _____

2 She _____

3 It was _____

4 You _____

5 They had _____

6 We have _____

7 I _____

8 They have _____

9 They were _____

10 We _____

(B) Write the word that fills each space.

1 The teacher _____ each child a new pencil.

2 Each child was _____ a new pencil.

3 All the pens were _____ out.

4 Ann has _____ Beth a sweet.

5 Terry _____ me a big red apple.

6 Jennifer _____ her mother a kiss before going to bed.

7 Every child at the party will be _____ a toy.

8 Wai was sorry that she had _____ all her sweets away.

9 Harjit liked the bat that Uncle Yusuf _____ him.

SIMILES

When something is very light in weight we say it is **as light as a feather**.

This is because a feather is so very, very light.

Learn the sayings in the list below.

as black as pitch   *as hot as fire*
as brown as a berry   *as soft as putty*
as easy as A B C   *as sour as vinegar*
as green as grass   *as stiff as a poker*
as hard as nails   *as weak as a kitten*

(A) Write the missing words.

   1 as weak as a _____   **6** as hard as _____
   2 as sour as _____   **7** as stiff as a _____
   3 as easy as _____   **8** as soft as _____
   4 as brown as a _____   **9** as black as _____
   5 as green as _____   **10** as hot as _____

(B) Now think of some new comparisons and
   avoid using the sayings above.

   1 as black as _____
   2 as easy as _____
   3 as difficult as _____
   4 as hot as _____
   5 as happy as _____

(C) Complete these sentences.
   Use comparisons so descriptive and so
   convincing that your reader knows exactly
   how you felt when each incident happened.

   1 The vicious cat's claws sank into my arm
      like _____
   2 When I told my mother the news, she
      turned as pale as _____
   3 When I had to read in assembly, my heart
      was beating like _____
   4 I was so frightened that my stomach felt
      as if _____

OPPOSITES USING *un-,in-,im-*

The **opposite** of certain adjectives can be formed by adding **un-**, **in-**, or **im-**.

Adding un-		Adding in- or im-	
certain	uncertain	capable	incapable
comfortable	uncomfortable	complete	incomplete
common	uncommon	convenient	inconvenient
conscious	unconscious	correct	incorrect
healthy	unhealthy	curable	incurable
pleasant	unpleasant	direct	indirect
selfish	unselfish	secure	insecure
steady	unsteady	sufficient	insufficient
suitable	unsuitable	visible	invisible
truthful	untruthful	movable	immovable
used	unused	possible	impossible
wise	unwise	pure	impure

(A) Write the opposites of these adjectives.

1 secure	**6** certain	**11** sufficient	**16** steady
2 selfish	**7** direct	**12** healthy	**17** possible
3 pure	**8** pleasant	**13** movable	**18** suitable
4 common	**9** convenient	**14** used	**19** wise
5 capable	**10** correct	**15** visible	**20** complete

(B) Use your dictionary and decide which adjective in the lists of opposites best describes:

1 a person who frequently tells lies
2 a salary that is not enough to live on
3 something that cannot be seen
4 a person who is frequently ill
5 a person who puts others before himself
6 a pack of cards from which some are missing
7 a rock that cannot be moved
8 a disease that cannot be cured
9 a sum in which there is a mistake
10 a person who has fainted

USING ADJECTIVES

The man walked down the road.

*The **old** man walked down the road.*

Sentence 2 is better than sentence 1 because it tells us something about the man. He was **old**. **Old is an adjective**.

*The **old** man walked down the **dusty** road.*

This is better than either 1 or 2 because it also tells us something about the road. It was **dusty**. **Dusty is also an adjective**.

Here are more adjectives:

angry	cold	foggy	lovely	ripe
blazing	cosy	frightened	naughty	savage
brave	damaged	hungry	nearby	stormy
clever	delicious	kind	pretty	straying

(A) Copy these sentences, filling each space with a suitable adjective from the list above.

1 The _____ girl wore a _____ dress.
2 The _____ huntsman enjoyed the _____ dinner.
3 A _____ dog was snarling at the _____ boy.
4 It was a _____ night.
5 The _____ sailor dived into the _____ sea to save his mate.
6 The pear was perfectly _____.
7 There was a _____ fire in the _____ kitchen.
8 The _____ car was towed to a _____ garage.
9 The _____ sheepdog rounded up the _____ sheep.
10 The _____ father punished his _____ son.

(B) Make sentences of your own from these words, putting two adjectives in each.

1 man; won; prize
2 baby; played; rattle
3 sun; shone; sky
4 ship; wrecked; shore
5 shopkeeper; served; customer
6 cat; chased; mouse

(C) Complete these sentences.

1 The shy girl _____
2 The blazing sun _____
3 The noisy car _____
4 The slimy creature _____

THE FAITHFUL COLLIE

James Hogg was a well-known poet, but he was also a shepherd. One night, when he was out with his sheep, it started to snow heavily. Knowing that he would have to get his flock in, Hogg whistled for his faithful collie. When she came running to him, he told her to get all the sheep in from one side of the moor while he did the same on the other side. Off they both went.

The shepherd returned much later, bringing with him the sheep he had rounded up. As there was no sign of the collie, he went into his cabin to wait.

After several hours a painful whine and a feeble scratching were heard at the door. Rushing out, the shepherd saw that the collie had brought in her share of the flock with not a single sheep missing. Then he noticed that the collie carried something in her mouth. He called her and she came and laid at his feet a new-born puppy.

Off she went into the snow again, but soon returned with another puppy, but as she took this to her master she fell to the ground and died. James Hogg knew that although his faithful collie had had her puppies in a snowstorm she had carried out her duty to her master and had brought the sheep safely home.

1 What work did James Hogg do besides writing poetry?

2 What happened when he was out with his sheep one night?

3 How did the shepherd call his collie?

4 What did he tell her to do?

5 What did the shepherd do when he returned with the sheep?

6 What did he hear at the door of his cabin after waiting for several hours?

7 What did he see when he rushed out?

8 Continue the story. Write six more sentences saying what James Hogg did next and how he felt.